*The Art
of
Self-Fulfillment*

Dr. Morton Litwack
&
Miriam Roher Resnick

The Art
of
Self-Fulfillment

YOU CAN TAKE CHARGE OF YOUR LIFE

Cornerstone Library
Published by Simon & Schuster, Inc. ● New York

Copyright © 1984 by Dr. Morton Litwack
and Miriam Roher Resnick
All rights reserved
including the right of reproduction
in whole or in part in any form
Published by Cornerstone Library
A Division of Simon & Schuster, Inc.
Simon & Schuster Building
Rockefeller Center
1230 Avenue of the Americas
New York, New York 10020

CORNERSTONE LIBRARY and colophon are registered trademarks of
Simon & Schuster, Inc.

10 9 8 7 6 5 4 3 2 1

Manufactured in the United States of America

Library of Congress Cataloging in Publication Data

Litwack, Morton.
    The art of self-fulfillment.

    1. Self-actualization (Psychology)   2. Self-
actualization (Psychology)—Problems, exercises, etc.
I. Resnick, Miriam Roher.   II. Title.
BF637.S4L57   1984   158'.1   83-25178

ISBN: 0-346-16005-7

To
Shasta and Sydney
who are essential to our own self-fulfillment

Contents

The Collaborator's Confession

When Dr. Morton Litwack and I first sat down together to discuss this book (we had been referred to each other by Alice Sicular, a mutual friend) I was feeling more than a little skeptical. My doubts had nothing to do with the fact that Dr. Litwack was a professor, a management development consultant, and a professional counselor, but not a writer. After all, I myself am a professional writer and I had at that time written several successful books with other experts who, like Dr. Litwack, were neophytes in the tough area of book-length publishing.

It was Dr. Litwack's premise that bothered me.

What made him think that he could possibly teach people how to solve their problems by themselves, without benefit of a trained intermediary sitting across a desk or at the head of a couch? Could anyone really be instructed, in a book, how to snatch the elusive insights and to glean the equally elusive life-saving advice that professional clinical psychologists get good money to provide for troubled individuals? Only the magician knows where the rabbit is hidden. That's a *given*. Who could possibly make us all magicians, even in the space of a whole book?

I got the answer in a very simple fashion. Dr. Litwack handed me the tools—the varied exercises now described in these pages—and told me to try them out on myself. (He did hint that it would be no violation of the ground rules if I mentioned the nature of my personal problems to him, but I weaseled out. He was, after all, only a prospective collaborator, not my minister.)

Using Dr. Litwack's psychological maps and instruments, I set myself (now I was eager) to confront some real challenges: long-standing, even lifetime bumps and potholes in the path of my life, annoyances and sorrows and difficulties that I had learned to tolerate and to which I had become resigned, though never really reconciled. When you've had the same hang-up for 30 years, you tend to take your suffering for granted, like an allergy.

I was still skeptical, but I wanted to give the man a chance. So I did what I was told. I wrote the requisite paragraphs, feeling liberated that I didn't need to write whole sentences because nobody would ever read them but me. I administered to myself the necessary questionnaires. I put myself in front of an imaginary video screen. I asked myself the prescribed leading questions. I made lists, as per directions. I gave rein to my insufficiently used creative right brain and let myself fantasize. And I also listened attentively, with an increasing feeling of amazement, when Dr. Litwack reeled off case histories illustrating so many different kinds of other people's problems that I inevitably saw, attached to other (made-up) names, my own familiar sorrows.

Dr. Litwack and I put all this in the context of nine chapters and it was like peeling a multi-skinned onion. One layer of the protective skin that masks personal reality came off in Chapter 2. Another layer was removed in Chapter 3. Yet another in the fourth chapter. By Chapter 9, the mysterious problems of my life were laid bare to me and the solutions to my personal misconceptions and hang-ups were revealed in all their newly perceived simplicity. I had a fresh outlook on some painful aspects of my personal life. And I also had a new coauthor and a new book.

It has been a joy to help make this work a reality and thus to share (thanks to the valued complicity of our agent, Sue Bartczak) all my recently gained insights with the rest of the population. I think I hit the jackpot. And so will you.

Miriam Roher Resnick
(for the team of
Litwack and Resnick)

I

Are You Satisfied With Your Life?

ARE YOU "HAPPY"? Most people are not, though they might deny it. Their daily lives nag at them. Free-floating anxiety disturbs their sleep. The job. The bills. The wife. The girlfriend. The husband. The lover. The loneliness. The children. The elderly parent. The loud music next door. The state of the world. Fears of death, or illness, of being mugged, or fired, or laid off. General unease. Is this the inescapable human condition?

What is happiness and what makes people happy? Some believe happiness is made of money. Or finding the right mate. Or fame, success, or possessions. But in real life, none of these necessarily constitutes happiness.

Each can and does bring associated problems. The course of true love seldom runs smooth, as we all know. Money and possessions bring anxieties. Fame invades privacy and could lead to assassination. When priests or ministers or rabbis decry worldly things as life's single goal, they know what they are talking about. They see too many troubled souls in the course of their ministries. Many of those troubled souls are rich and successful and well mated.

The truth is, of course, that nobody is happy all the time, not even a small child who hasn't lived long enough to know about money or ambition or sex. And yet some individuals enjoy a basic serenity that persists over long periods. They are "together," to use the current jargon. They seem to have accepted themselves. They cope, without panic, with the minor crises of day-to-day life. They even deal competently with disaster. They sorrow, they mourn, then they achieve recovery and reorder their personal worlds with bravery and even humor.

What makes the difference between chronically troubled individuals and those who can deal successfully and often happily with their lives?

The answer is no secret to those scholars who have studied the human psyche. Their names constitute an honor roll of the sciences of human behavior: Freud, Jung, and Adler, of course. But also Erik Erikson, Carl Rogers, Abraham Maslow, and numerous other social scientists. They have all delved into the mysteries of the spirit that underlie our outer selves to find out why we behave and feel the way we do. They have discovered that each of us is not one person but at least two and even more: the outer selves and the inner selves.

The outer selves are the "public" individuals who deal (sometimes poorly) with the world. The inner selves are the often very different individuals who dwell within us. We may be unaware of these power-ful subconscious influences. But they may nevertheless cause internal debates, disagreements, and battles. Such conflicts not only make us feel unhappy but also make it difficult to solve the problems of daily life and to reach the decisions necessary to resolve those problems.

When we feel one way on the inside but act another way on the outside, the sense of confusion and impotence can be devastating. But when the inner and outer selves come to understanding and construc-tive compromise, we are made whole, serene, happy, and fulfilled.

We make our own difficulties

Long ago, acting on the theory that each of us harbors at least one buried self, Freud devised a means of treating and helping troubled individuals who are dissatisfied, sometimes acutely so, with their lives. The "talking" therapy Freud used was essentially a means of helping his patients get in touch with their inner selves. His method has been utilized, with refinements and variations, by tens of thousands of psychiatrists, psychoanalysts, psychologists, mental health counselors, and pastors all over the Western world for the last hundred years.

And yet relatively few troubled people avail themselves of the help that these mental health practitioners can provide. For one thing, most such professional help is expensive. Often the process is one-on-one. One troubled person, one counselor, an hour at a time, one or more times a week for weeks or months or even years. For another thing, most of us do not elevate our chronic unhappiness to the status of an illness that needs to be treated by a professional. We take our ailing autos to a trained mechanic. But our personal problems do not seem acute enough to go to a specialist. After all, most of us are not tempted to shoot ourselves or somebody else. We get along, somehow. "So I'm not happy," we tell ourselves. "So what? Is anybody?" And we limp along from day to day in a more or less constant state of unease, barely coping, just enduring.

The pity of it is that this low-key suffering need not be. It is within the capability of most of us to get to the root of many of our problems without resorting to outside help. The clues to our difficulties lie within ourselves, in our failure to establish good communication be-tween the selves that cry for recognition within us, and the selves we have fabricated to meet the world. *Most of our difficulties are of our own making.* Once we understand what we are doing to ourselves, we have a good chance of understanding how to attain self-fulfillment, to find our real selves.

"I have a little shadow"

"Find my real self? I know who I am!"

But do you, really? Actually, you have many selves. One of you is the person who leaves the house in the morning to go to work or to face the neighbors and the world in general. Another is the individual who lives with wife or husband. Yet another is your children's parent. And a different one is the social person — the individual on a date, or at a party, playing tennis or racquetball. These are the facades you present that fool everybody else and sometimes even yourself.

Have you ever thought, as you walked into an office or a party or a classroom or even into the home or workplace of an acquaintance or customer: "Oh, if they really knew how I feel, would they be surprised!"?

We know (sometimes not consciously, but we do know it, somewhere inside) that we are playing a role, that this is our public manifestation. We are dressed to create a particular impression. We talk in such a way as to reinforce that impression. Our behavior conforms to the same role. Maybe that role is competent executive. Or devoted wife and mother. Or hotshot salesman. Or man of the world. We may want people to think we are a devil-may-care nonconformist. Or a pillar of the community. Or a carefree big spender. Or a sober lawyer. Or several of these, at various times.

But inside we are somebody else. A failure. A hurt child. A thwarted lover. A person who messes up. A fraud. And the conflict between the various personae—inside, outside—is the cause of most of our unhappiness.

For example

Here are some real-life examples.

1. Sam is a 37-year-old computer scientist who worked for a major corporation. Now he is a free-lance consultant, well thought of, much in demand. And yet he is unhappy. He has trouble winding up his assignments. He is forever looking for more and more data. He is never convinced that he has enough information about a given problem. Therefore, he has immense difficulty in writing a final

report. He keeps putting it off. He is, he thinks, a natural-born procrastinator. He keeps bothering his clients for more facts, to the point that they feel pestered and annoyed. Sam is aware that he is not turning out work in relation to his ability. He feels frustrated, driven, and unhappy.

2. Marge is 45. She has always been a capable homemaker and a conscientious mother. But now her children are grown and homemaking is not enough to interest her. She would love to get a job but she is afraid to even start looking. She is painfully shy and depends almost entirely on her husband for making contact with the outside world. So her job hunt is stalled. She believes society doesn't offer opportunities for women like her. She feels she might as well resign herself to staying home because no one would hire her anyway. But she is so bored and unhappy. She feels like a nothing.

3. Jean is a reasonably attractive 27-year-old editor on the staff of a technical magazine. Those she works with see her as capable and pleasant and in her professional relationships she is more than adequate. But in social situations she is cold and quiet. Her social life is devoid of men. She is aching to form a relationship and eventually to get married. But nobody seems interested in her.

"Beyond my control"

What Sam and Marge and Jean all have in common—though their problems are very different—is a conviction that their troubles are beyond their control. We all share this conviction at one time or another. What can you possibly do about a death in the family, or a lost job, or race prejudice, or a falling stock market, or an unfaithful wife, or ... or ...?

It goes without saying that external events are frequently beyond the control of any individual or his or her minister, counselor, or doctor. Even one's financial adviser cannot prevent the stock market from taking an inconvenient plunge. But it is also true that many of us unreasonably blame outside circumstances for our failures and our misery.

"I got divorced because my wife couldn't get along with anybody, not only me."

"I was fired because my boss simply didn't like me."

"Sure I failed the course. The teacher didn't explain anything and so I couldn't understand the material."

True enough, perhaps, but what part did *you* play in the failure?

Other explanations for the same disasters could be:

"I decided on divorce because part of me really didn't want to be married anymore."

"My boss reminded me of an uncle I can't stand. So I treated the boss the way I wanted to treat my uncle. And I got fired."

"The truth is that I wasn't listening most of the time. I don't know what the teacher said. So I failed the exam."

Not all personal failures are related to our internal selves. But both our internal selves and our external selves deal with external events and have a great deal to do with the outcome.

That inner voice

Consider Sam, the computer scientist who could hardly bring himself to stop amassing data and to submit a finished report. His problem is that he doesn't trust himself. Another Sam nags at him:

"You're not good enough. You really aren't such a hotshot. You are actually a bit of a fraud. You must keep on working. If you avoid finishing your report, people won't find out how inadequate you are."

Sam needs to face his inner self and find out why that nagging persona doesn't trust the capable consultant the world sees. He is his own worst enemy.

As for Marge, the depressed wife, her problem, too, is at least partly within herself. Of course, it is difficult for a homemaker to make the transition to the business world. But the real stumbling block is that inner self who tells her not to expose herself to rejection. A timid, shy girl is Marge's other self. "Don't hurt me!" cries the girl to the middle-aged adult. Once Marge recognizes and comes to terms with that frightened youngster within her, finds out why she is so afraid, she will be able to work out a way of freeing herself to seek a fuller life.

As for Jean, the cool, competent but still single career woman: short of an arranged marriage (which doesn't happen any more in our society) Jean will never find her true love unless she becomes fully aware of the inner Jean. That hidden self learned long ago from her parents that she was the ugly, awkward sister who had only one saving grace, a brilliant mind. As a result, the grown-up Jean feels unworthy except in a working situation. But once Jean deals with that outworn perception of herself, she will no longer fear to reveal herself to eligible men.

Clearly, all three of these people — Sam, Marge, and Jean — are blocking their own self-fulfillment. They are unable to act because someone "inside" is throwing obstacles in their way.

Now let us consider three others (also real people) who seem to have removed the roadblocks by achieving harmonious relationships among their various selves.

Unschackled

1. Sandy, divorced, 37, is the mother of two children. She has been single for three years and has been involved with another man for over a year. The happy side of this romance is that both are truly in love with each other. The unhappy, flip side is that it has been impossible for the two to get along well on a day-to-day basis. Sandy cannot endure his unreliability. He cannot put up with Sandy's incessant criticism.

   Then Sandy consults her inner self. She realizes that at her age it is important for her to establish a permanent relationship. This need transcends her need for a flaming physical romance. And so, reluctantly but courageously, Sandy has told her lover that she believes the relationship will not last. Now she is beginning to see other men to find someone who will meet her deep-seated other needs. It hasn't been easy—but Sandy is able to make a clear-eyed, reasoned choice among her own alternatives.

2. Phil is a 30-year-old who several years ago actually enjoyed law school as an intellectual challenge and who easily passed the bar exam. And yet for three years he was unable to find a legal position in the large city that was his home. He told his parents, who had footed the bill for his expensive education, that he doubted he was cut out to be an attorney. Miserably, he felt he had failed to meet their reasonable expectations.

   Suddenly, Phil announced a new decision. He would seek a job in a smallish agricultural community several hundred miles away from home. Within a month, he had secured a legal position with a public agency in that small city. Soon he became so successful and well thought of that he was even being considered for a judgeship.

   At long last, Phil had come to terms with his inner self. He realized he could not take the pressures of private big-time law practice in a metropolitan area. He had failed to get a job because he really didn't want a job. But the low-pressure situation in a smaller city, working for local government, was so relaxing for him that it made up for the loss of theater, symphony, and other delights of the big city. He was able to put aside his parent's expectations and consider his own inner needs.

3. Sharon, a free-lance writer for magazines, gave up her professional career when she married in the 1950s and had children. She tried to assuage her misery at being confined to the company of babies. She became a community activist, working hard as a volunteer in half a dozen do-good causes and even running for local office. But the added activities only brought frustrations and tension. Eventually, Sharon came to realize that writing had always been what she wanted to do—solitary, creative, and, for her, relaxing. So she brushed aside her own excuses that she had lost her professional contacts. She started a new career as a writer of fiction, gave up all her board positions, and lost her incipient ulcer.

All three of these people were able to slough off the demands and arbitrary rules made by parents, social pressure, and spouses, and accepted by their conscious selves. Their guidelines had been what was expected of them by others, not what fulfilled their own deepest needs. But all three recognized, after a period of anguish and unhappiness, their unique personal requirements. They came to realize that they were not necessarily locked into the status quo. Rather, they saw alternatives and were able to make viable decisions about how to conduct their lives. In psychological terms, they became actualized: living up to their own potential abilities, using their own special intellectual and spiritual resources to make a self-fulfilling life.

If an analyst were to interview these individuals in depth, he or she would find that they have given up their childish illusions about what life is like: they see things as they really are. Somehow, they became able to size up a life problem, to consider the options, and then to choose a course that had the best chance of realizing their goals—be those goals marital, professional, social, recreational, or parental. They were also able to settle for less if, realistically, less was the only available option. People like these are proactive—they take the initiative—rather than reactive—waiting for circumstances to push them into doing something. They use as many of their individual resources as they can possibly muster to meet life's challenges. Even if the outcome is not always totally satisfactory, they have the satisfaction of knowing they have done their best, to the limit of their ability. Such people have found self-fulfillment. And you can do it too.

Do-it-yourself

Some people whose lives are not going well consult psychiatrists, psychologists, and professional counselors. But they seldom take that step unless they are feeling such extreme distress that they literally can no longer function. Some troubled individuals even seek medical advice: it is well known that emotional distress often manifests itself as physical illness. It is also true that most illnesses are affected (either positively or negatively) by one's emotional state and mental attitude.

Nevertheless, most of those who are discontented or chronically unhappy or frustrated never seek any kind of professional help. They feel like Job, whose burdens came from God. "This is the way it is for me," they say to themselves. "I'm unlucky but I can't change it, any more than I can change the color of my eyes or skin, any more than I can grow six inches taller or make myself shorter. That's how it is. Sigh! Sigh!"

What they do not realize is that change and solutions are within themselves. Everyone has alternatives, no matter what the problem.

You may have a failed marriage—but you can come to understand, by consulting your inner selves, why the marriage fell apart and how to work to prevent another marital disaster.

You may have a frustrating career situation—but you can devise a solution by getting to know your own half-hidden spirit. You will understand why you are having such difficulties and whether you need to change your approach or change your job.

You may be a grieving widow who truly believes that life is now over for you. And yet you can find inner resources that will help you construct a new life on the wreckage of the old one.

Whatever your discontent, you can, indeed, find ways of coping, if you know how and where to look.

How is it done? That is what this book is all about.

The technique

The technique of finding self-fulfillment is not new. It was pioneered by Freud and all his illustrious successors. In recent years, much simpler variants of the same basic procedures have been devised by specialists in human development.

For example, Ira Progoff has helped people gain new insights through their own writing. Milton H. Erickson has found powerful ways of communicating with the unconscious through hypnosis.

Richard Bandler and John Grinder have developed neurolinguistic programming, a way of communicating with one's inner self, using a combination of hypnosis, language, and counseling strategies. Sidney Simon has contributed greatly to the technique of values clarification.

John Lilly has developed the useful concept that each of us constructs his or her own reality; whatever we believe to be true, *is* true. Jack R. Gibb has devised exercises and other approaches to the key personal problem of self-trust. Moshe Feldenkrais has pioneered in mind-body relationships, showing the strong connection between bodily attributes and mental attitudes. These various approaches, among others, are being successfully used by thousands of psychologists and counselors.

The good news, now, is that a troubled person need not necessarily consult a professional to set in motion these techniques for creating personal harmony. In the chapters to come, we will explain how to use the techniques that have been shown to be effective in the process of self-analysis and self-examination.

In the pages that follow we will describe typical personal problems that cause people to be unhappy. We will analyze each of these problems and show how these individuals created their own difficulties— and then were able to come to terms with them in order to become truly self-fulfilled. Then we will provide simple exercises that you can do yourself that will help you to identify the exact nature of your own problem. (Let us reemphasize that many of us think we are unhappy about one thing when the trouble is really something quite different.) Succeeding chapters will describe how you can reach within yourself to get in touch with what has thus far been hidden. Hypnosis is not involved, just pencil-and-paper work and guided self-analysis. The next part of the process is negotiation, learning how to reach agreement with various parts of yourself, the conscious and the heretofore unheeded unconscious.

From all this, a course of action will emerge, one that takes into consideration all those selves that constitute YOU. It will not bring the dead back to life. It will make no change in your boss or your lover or your parent. But your feelings and attitudes will be different. Your approach to the circumstances of your life will be changed. It is also possible that you will be led to new ways of living your life. You may decide to marry, or to change jobs, or to go to work. Or join a new group. Or take a trip. Or retire. Or move to California. Whatever the decision, it will be made by agreement of all of your selves. It will be a happy decision, a firm step ahead in the journey of your own life.

The examined life

Socrates wisely remarked that the unexamined life is not worth living. In fact, without examination, life cannot be fully lived.

Do you need to examine your life? Are you getting in the way of your own fulfillment? Here are some of the symptoms:

Do you find that part of you wants to do one thing and part of you wants to do another?

Do you have trouble making even small decisions?

Are you dissatisfied with your efforts, even though you have tried very hard to do well?

Do you feel chronically anxious, worried, or angry, and not really sure what you are so worried or anxious or angry about?

Do you make commitments and then have difficulty forcing yourself to do what you said you would do?

Do you feel that you have unused potential, and yet have been unable to live up to your own expectations and abilities?

All these are signs that you have set up your own obstacles.

Whatever your problem, you need to get in touch with your various inner selves and find out why you are stalled, braked, conflicted, immobilized, worried, or depressed. You need to ask yourself the right questions so that you can nail down your real problems (in contrast to the problems you think you have). Once you have consulted yourselves, called a "family" meeting, you will be in a position to harmonize "family" relationships. A process of continuing communication can be set in motion. After that, the solution of your real problems will be well on the way. None of this is easy. But it is the path to becoming "happy"—self-fulfilled, self-actualized. And you can do it yourself.

Read on.

2

*Pinpointing
Your
Problems*

"SO HOW ARE THINGS going with you these days?"

This is the homely question that one counselor usually asks a new client after he or she is settled in the chair facing him. The answer is apt to be hesitant, maybe "Oh, well, I don't know. I just. . . ." And then there is a new, unspoken question, a continuing hesitancy. It is as if the person who has come for help with personal problems doubts that anyone would really be interested in what is troubling him or her. "Nobody cares but me!" hangs in the air.

Any skilled professional knows how to deal with this familiar diffidence. One or two leading remarks, a few more gentle questions, and the client is pouring it all out, usually with a flood of tears. Even men (trained not to do so) also cry. Deep feelings and painful memories are being exposed. And so the process of pinpointing one's problems and seeking their solutions is launched.

Can you do that by yourself? Can you give yourself the luxury, enjoy the infinite relief, of paying attention to yourself? Normally, we are like machines, programmed by habit to do our jobs, to give a certain amount of consideration to our family and friends, to follow routine in work and in recreation. Even when the machinery of our lives develops alarming noises, gives signs of needing repairs or rehabilitation, we find ourselves doggedly continuing the same daily habits, locked in by what is, afraid to take a look at what could be. We put down unease and feelings that something could be wrong. We hide our troubles from others. Worse, we try to hide our troubles from ourselves. The effort to keep aloft the "business as usual" banner gets more and more burdensome.

What a relief it would be to let the banner drop, to allow all our rebellious, unhappy feelings to show for a change! What a luxury to let it all hang out! But who would listen?

Consider the man who took a solitary trip to Australia in a 15½-foot boat. He was interviewed on a morning television show. The host of the program asked him how he coped with loneliness on the long voyage. "Oh," said the adventurer, "that was never a problem. I had an imaginary friend I talked to the whole time. That friend was a great listener! Together we dealt with everything that happened during the trip."

A friend is a counselor

Many people derive great benefit from talking things over with real friends. They air their frustrations, their joys, whatever in their lives is currently preoccupying them. In such a relationship, the friend may comment on what is being confided but might just make sympathetic sounds. It is not the friend's reactions that necessarily help, though some of us do have extremely wise close friends. The value of such a dialogue or (actually) monologue is that, by the very act of putting concerns into words, a person seems to get insights into problems that previously escaped him or her. Somehow, describing your circumstances seems to shed light and to suggest solutions that have not previously occurred to you.

Talking things over with a sympathetic listener causes matters to come clear that were previously hazy. Instead of turning a deaf ear to those still small voices that speak to you during wakeful moments in the night, you finally listen. You acknowledge your feelings, feelings that represent information you have collected but suppressed, valuable data that suddenly is transformed into "I always knew. . . ."

Each of us has, within us, a storehouse of such information, collected during all the years of our lives. This is data that could show us how to free ourselves from current miseries, if only we knew how to bring it out and examine it at long last.

How can one open these hidden files? Some people go to hypnotists, who are expert at dredging out the secrets of the unconscious. Some go to counselors who know how to ask leading questions. Some speak to good friends. And some resort to imaginary friends, as the solitary long-distance sailor did. That method is more direct, costs no money, and could be as effective as any other.

You, too, can have your own imaginary friend. Many already have one. Remember your friend when you were a child? You talked constantly to a doll. Or to a stuffed animal. Or to a made-up individual with an unlikely name, like Xerox or Mr. Kakoya or Judy Thimble. Many adults talk to their dogs or cats. The deeply religious speak to God, Jesus, Moses, a patron saint. You could confide in any of those now. Or, you could talk it all over with your own inner child, that vulnerable, defenseless creature who suffered long-ago hurts and fears, misunderstandings and losses, as well as joys, triumphs, and loves, strong feelings that echo within the adult You to this very day.

Tell your inner child, who knows how it all started. Tell your friend, who cares, what is going on in your life today. You might start with: "What a frustrating day I had. . . ." The conversation with your friend will pay off. It will lead you to discover what your problems really are.

A problem well-defined

You already know what your problems are? The fact is that you probably do not know. A problem well-defined is a problem partly solved. If you are struggling helplessly, the chances are that you do not really understand your problem.

Why do so many of us stew in our own juices, thrash around in the quicksand of seemingly insoluble dilemmas, never seem to see the light at the end of the tunnel? The reason often is that we have failed to come to grips with the true nature of our difficulties. We fight straw men, while the real opponents are sniping at us with actual bullets just outside our line of vision. We don't know what ails us and we try to medicate the wrong symptoms.

Here are some examples.

1. A businessman struggled through four successive partnerships. Each one broke up with recriminations and bad feelings. He was in despair. The nature of his business was such that a partner was essential. "Why am I such a poor judge of people?" he asked himself. "Why do I have such a genius for choosing the wrong partners?"

   But the problem was not what he thought. His real problem was that he expected too much of people, not only his partners but also his wife, his children, his friends, his employees. Everyone was always disappointing him. He wanted everybody to behave just the way he did. He gave no one any room for individuality or priorities different from his own. Once his problem was realistically restated, he was halfway to a solution.

2. A 40-year-old woman felt as if her life had turned to ashes. She and her successful attorney husband were always at odds, over money, over the way their teenage children should be brought up, over her housekeeping, over their social life. She wanted to go back to the university and get a master's degree to prepare herself for a job, so she could get away from home and the misery it represented. But her husband made it clear that she would not be successful there either. So she felt like a failure in every aspect of her life.

   This woman blamed herself for everything that was distressing in her situation. Her husband treated her as inferior and she had come to accept his assessment. But, in truth, she was actually both competent and intelligent. Indeed, 18 years earlier she had graduated from college with honors. Her real problem was a low self-image, aggravated by the many years during which she and her mate struggled for power and he won by means of his campaign of belittlement. For a sense of security, she had bartered away almost all that remained of her sense of self-worth. That was her real problem.

3. According to an elementary school teacher, her problem was her work. "I talk to little kids all day long. It's driving me crazy!" she cried. "I need another job. The trouble is, I'm not trained to do anything else." But boredom with teaching was not this young woman's real problem. Rather, her problem was loneliness. She needed to see herself as a person who could relate to adults as well as children. Her task was to learn how to release the adult buried within her, to emerge from the shell of self-deprecation she had grown around herself, to get herself into the frame of mind to seek out other adults—in a club, in church, in a hiking group, even on the bus.

Think of the people you know. You can spot other ill-defined problems. The person who thinks he is a procrastinator but whose real difficulty is lack of confidence. The individual who is struggling with shyness but who is really afraid to talk to people lest they find out that he is smarter than everybody else. The woman who thinks she could lose pounds if only she didn't eat so much but whose real problem is the habit of rewarding herself with food to compensate for frustration. These are only a few examples of people who are not facing up to their real problems. Anyone can think of others by considering the difficulties of friends and relatives.

What is the moral of these real life stories?

Awareness precedes change

Awareness must come before change. You may be miserable. You may be on the horns of a dilemma. You may feel trapped. You may be having terrible trouble with a wife, a husband, a child, a boss. You may have lost a beloved spouse or your job or your health. You may be bored, or lonely, or just generally unhappy. Whatever your apparent problem, do you know what your real problem is? What is behind it all? Only if you are aware of the real problem can you take constructive steps to solve it.

The good news is that there are ways of developing awareness and of identifying the real problem with the help of your own best friend:

your inner self. The human mind is a perfect recorder of everything that has happened in one's life. By opening this encyclopedia we each carry around, we can discover not only the true nature of our difficulties but also clues to their solution.

The unconscious mind is always trying to take care of us, in dreams, in daydreams, in wakeful moments during the night. All too frequently, we fail to listen. But a deliberate dialogue with that inner self, that handy, faithful friend, will reveal information that the conscious mind has been suppressing.

It is remarkable, but true, that there are no irrelevancies in the unconscious. All our past experiences have something to say about the life we lead today. If you take the time and have the patience to get in touch with your inner self, your unconscious will inevitably lead you to valuable insights about your current problem(s). You could be wrong about the precise nature of the difficulty you seek to overcome. On the other hand, you could be quite right. In either case, if you open yourself to what your unconscious knows, you will find out not only the nature of your problem but also how to solve it.

Even if you have already put a label on your problem, you could be mistaken. You could have decided that

I have an inferiority complex.
I am insecure.
I am depressed.

Forget it. Most labels are as misleading as a road sign that has been turned in the opposite direction by youthful pranksters. Perhaps you do have an inferiority complex. But you might just possibly be suffering from the reverse: you may really think you're better than everybody else. You might label yourself insecure—but everybody is insecure about something. You're depressed? It's only because you're running around in circles chasing the tail of your problem. Capture the problem itself and you probably won't be depressed any more.

Make a list

Make a list of your problems as you now see them. If you are lucky, your list will be brief. Here is a sampling.

Now that the children have left home, they hardly ever phone. They don't seem to care about me.

I'm getting nowhere in my job but I'm stuck with it.

I'm sick of my friends.

I think my husband is playing around.

We fight all the time.

My life is over since my wife died.

I'm not attractive to men (women).

Why am I having so much trouble learning this stuff? I can't seem to concentrate.

I have a terrible memory.

I worry about money all the time.

I'm a procrastinator and it's getting me into trouble.

All the romance is gone from my marriage.

I need a different job.

Have you made your own list? Now talk about it to your imaginary friend. Don't be self-conscious. There are ways of communicating that don't lead to social embarrassment. This is how you do it:

Your life is a book

Put your list of problems aside. You will use them later. But now you are assigned to imagine your life as a book. Start at the back of the book, by thinking about the current chapter first. Meditate on what is going on in your life. Then think about the previous chapter. Work your way back to the chapter that deals with your childhood.

Have you finished remembering? Now write five paragraphs that will be seen by no one but you and your imaginary friend. Don't worry about sentence structure or spelling. Don't care about grammar. Don't bother with beautiful language. This is for your eyes alone. If you know enough English to read this book, you know more than enough to write short paragraphs about the subject you know best: your own life.

The paragraphs are to deal with the following subjects, one topic to each paragraph: My daily life. My physical self. Me and the community. Significant happenings in my past. Others in my life.

Write anything that comes into your head. Do it like a daydream. No rules. Just start each section with the key word and then, let 'er rip!

Are you still uncertain about what you are supposed to do? Here are five paragraphs set down by someone who was persuaded (after writing them in privacy) to allow them to be reproduced for the sake of this book. (The individual who wrote the paragraphs is a professional writer, so these musings might have a slightly more literary flavor than your own.)

My daily life. *My work is extremely important to my sense of well-being. Even when it doesn't go well, in a perverse way I enjoy the sense of frustration. Maybe because it proves I am alive and functioning and doing what I am peculiarly qualified to do. What a marvelous contrast with my "work" during those days when I was a volunteer. I was constantly frustrated, grappling with people who just wouldn't do what I thought they should do.*

Others in my life. *I think I've had more than my share of bad luck or bad judgment in my working life. People I've dealt with have not held up their end. The same is true of my brother. And my father. When the kids were little I used to tangle with them when we were preparing to go on a trip; all the work was left to me. It strikes me that my greatest problem is with people. I set high standards (I now realize) for how they should behave. And when they don't operate the way I think they should I get angry and upset. Who do I think I am, anyway?? I now realize my unrealistic attitude about people is a major problem for me.*

My physical self. *All my life I've had problems with my body. I was too short. Too clumsy and uncoordinated. Too skinny (as a child). I was the kid who was the last to be chosen for a team because I was just no good. When I try to do something with my hands I mess up. What does this mean? Am I really so uncoordinated or just inept because for some reason I never went to the trouble of learning how to do things? Another thing: I worry about illness a lot of the time. Usually the illness turns out to be imaginary. Why do I do that?*

Significant happenings in my past. *Being the top student in high school was the earliest highlight I can remember. My first date at 15 was so painful—a never-to-be-forgotten bad event. Testifying in divorce court about my uncle's marital breakup was terrible. My wedding—a happy memory. Watching my father die was awful. The children's birth—great events. Also their weddings. Getting my first book contract was an enormous high. I don't know what all this tells me. I don't see a pattern.*

Me and the community. *All my life I've thought of myself as a do-gooder. So many organizations, so many boards. In recent years I'm almost totally turned off all that. I'm on only one board now. I've become pretty cynical about what do-good organizations can accomplish and I'm thoroughly sick of meetings. I think people are in organizations to give themselves a sense of importance. That's probably why I did it all those years. I needed an outlet to get away from the house and the kids. Now that I have such great satisfaction in my work, I don't feel the need to do any of that any more. I suppose I really lived a fraudulent life when I was so occupied with saving society.*

Have you finished mentally reviewing the book of your own life? Next, write your own five paragraphs. Put down anything that comes to mind. Nobody will see this but you. (Rest assured that this system works. Similar techniques are used by well-known therapists. This is our own adaptation.)

What next?

Now that you have written your thoughts about the chief areas of your life, reread what you have put down. Read your words aloud (close the door) if you can persuade yourself to do so. (Only your imaginary friend is listening.) Let your mind drift, cued by the musings you have expressed on paper. If you have something to add now, add it. Have a conversation with your friend. Do you have some new thoughts about your problems? Do you want to revise your list?

Here was the original problems list of the individual who wrote the sample paragraphs:

I have bad luck with collaborators; they never deliver what they promise.

I have no physical coordination at all.

I feel guilty about dropping out of everything that's worthwhile.

I tend to be a hypochrondriac.

My brother doesn't do what he should to help with our mother.

But after the person had written the assigned paragraphs and thought about them, the list of problems changed:

I expect too much of people, not only professionally but also in personal life.

I try too hard in athletic activities, because I want to be "the top student" in all things. I think it makes me tense up and causes me to fail.

I feel a sense of guilt about doing anything I enjoy. Why?

Why do I worry about illness so much?

Internal vs. external

If you look over your own lists of problems—before writing the paragraphs, after writing the paragraphs—you will see that they can be divided another way: into internal problems or external problems. Labeling them that way is a useful thing to do. Examples of external problems are: A death in the family. Loss of a job. A difficult wife or husband or boss. Not enough money. Conditions at work. Illness. Accidents.

Here are some internal problems: Feeling of inferiority. Loneliness. Difficulty in dealing with people. A sense of insecurity. Perfectionism. Persistent feelings of guilt.

Of course, some problems are both internal and external, like a difficult boss with whom one doesn't know how to deal, or the need to care for a sick mother while feeling resentful about the burden. But if you do an honest job of labeling your own problems, you will see that in your revised list (compiled after writing the five paragraphs) every problem has an internal aspect.

Take, for example, the problem of a spouse's death. The internal problem in that external difficulty often is how to learn to be self-sufficient. Is the problem loss of a job? The internal problem might be figuring out what part you played in the failure and what, if anything, you should do about it. Have you a disappointing business associate or marital partner? The internal component could be to determine whether you are being realistic in your own attitudes and your own expectations.

Are you and your spouse fighting about money? Your mate's underlying internal problem may be a deep sense of insecurity, derived from an impoverished childhood. Your internal problem may be the attitude, learned from a parent on whom you have modeled yourself, that acquiring material things constitutes happiness. Your joint internal problem may be a struggle for power, the desire to dominate.

Whatever the nature of your problems, how you deal with the circumstances of your life has created those problems. Happily, your ability to solve the problems also lies within yourself. Hidden within each of us are infinite resources to cope with what happens to us during our lives. Uncovering those resources, finding our potential after years of disuse, is the way to play whatever hand we are dealt in the ongoing card game that is our own life.

State your priorities

Suppose your revised list includes four major problems that you think are preventing you from living a happy life. The number should not surprise you. No human being is without problems and most of us have several. True, there are times in all of our lives when we feel that things are going well, that life is full and beautiful. But it is not in the human condition to remain fulfilled and content. In every life there are good cycles and not-so-good cycles. Good times are replaced by bad and vice versa. The seasons change on earth and seasons change in our lives. We sometimes live, in Shakespeare's words, during the winter of our discontent. But in the natural course of things we will enjoy spring and, with luck, summer before fall.

What you must do now is to look through your current list of problems and not only determine the most pressing but also try to discern the pattern that runs through your difficulties. The interesting thing is that there undoubtedly is a pattern and your problems are probably all interrelated. Look hard. There is a pattern. Can you tell what it is?

Consider the revised problems list of the person who wrote our "sample" paragraphs. (See page 00.) The pattern is clear to any objective reader. This individual expects too much not only of self but of everybody. There is a striving for more than is humanly to be expected: of others, of body, of self. This is a highly competitive individual, an overachiever, doomed to multiple disappointments. The problem: how can she moderate her expectations, settle for less? Or is this person fated to suffer disappointment with self and everyone else throughout life?

Can you analyze your own list and find the recurrent theme of your life? The trick is to pretend that your list was made by someone else. In thinking about yourself, you have no perspective. So get a perspective by assuming, for the moment, the role of friend or counselor. Imagine that your list of problems was written by somebody you have never met. All you know about this person is written on the paper.

What is the underlying tendency of the individual whose problems are recited on the pages before you? What's the basic problem? Does this individual tend to expect too much, like our "model" paragraph writer? Is this person hung up on sex? Is a quest for security (and thus an underlying insecurity) the leitmotiv of this life? Is this the portrait of a little child, looking always for a mommy? Does the list show a person who fears rejection and thus constantly avoids situations that might lead to being disappointed and put down? Is this an anxious individual who is always creating imaginary difficulties?

These are all illustrations of how a person can actually get in his or her own way. By analyzing your list, you will emerge with an honest new view of yourself and how you are creating obstacles for yourself. Face facts realistically. You will learn that nobody dies of it.

For further illustration, let us return to the individual who expected too much of others and self. The person who wrote those paragraphs and came to understand that unrealistic expectations was a central life problem also came to understand that, having faced facts, it was possible to go right on living. Indeed, living became easier. All of a sudden, kindness became permissible, kindness to self and to others.

She thought: "Suppose I don't win the game? It won't kill me or anyone else. Suppose my brother dances less attention on mother than I do? Mother doesn't seem to be aware of it. Why should *I* care? Suppose the people in those organizations are in it for their own reasons—does that make the organization less worthy? Suppose I'm not perfect—is anybody? Suddenly it has become OK to feel affection for other people. They're imperfect, and so am I. Suddenly it has become OK to feel affection for myself. I share the human condition: imperfection."

For this person, as for you, now that the problem is stated, it is on the way to solution. One of the ways is to learn to trust yourself. Don't imagine that your new insight into your problem is all you have to do to achieve bliss. See the next chapter.

3

Do You Trust Yourself?

SEVERAL YEARS AGO a magazine ran a true life story with an unstated but powerful moral. It went something like this:

A young married couple had saved a little money, managed to buy a hilltop in a rural area, and built themselves, mostly with their own hands, a charming little home. But only a few months after the place was finished, disaster struck. It was a cold winter night. The couple had built a big fire in their fireplace. While they were dozing in front of the blaze, sparks from the unscreened fireplace ignited a conflagration in their living room. By the time they roused themselves, it was too late to save the home. It burned to the ground.

The loss was devastating. Distraught, the two young people went to see the husband's wealthy father and asked for a loan to enable them to reconstruct their house. The father amazed them by refusing.

"I trust you," he said, "to get the job done on your own. I'll be delighted to give you advice on how to go about getting a bank loan. I'll give you the benefit of my experience in the financial world. But I feel sure you can get your house rebuilt without my money."

What could the young peope do? Angry, disappointed, they were forced to swallow their resentment and take what the father offered: advice. They made the necessary arrangements and the necessary compromises. They stinted their daily lives to accomplish their goal. And the house was eventually rebuilt, with, of course, a new fire screen. The accomplishment was exhilarating. And they realized, belatedly, what a valuable gift the father had bestowed. His trust in their ability to contend with adversity on their own had forced them to trust themselves and to learn the true extent of their own resources. Their new house was all the more valuable to them because it was totally theirs, rebuilt without a parent's money.

Not one but several morals reside in this story. (1) Parents' overprotectiveness, so common among middle-class people, robs their children of the opportunity to learn to be self-reliant. (2) The trust of others is helpful in learning to trust oneself. (3) And self-trust makes possible the accomplishments and satisfactions that enrich our lives.

These principles apply to all of us. Any man or woman who is deficient in self-trust is making difficulties for him/herself. Lack of self-trust not only creates problems. It also makes it impossible to solve problems that exist.

Just what is self-trust?

Self-trust is composed of hunches. It is also intuition. It could be an insistent dream, or a sneaky feeling. It is an emotion that wells up.

Self-trust is also feeling good about something, maybe "for no reason at all," or feeling bad about something, also, perhaps, for no reason at all.

All these messages come from within. All provide significant data about the condition of one's life. All must be heeded and given due weight in our attempts to solve the problems of our lives. Sheer logic, unmixed with the basic truths of our own emotional requirements, is a poor basis for a marriage, or a career, or any other important life endeavor. That is why it is important to make the distinction between self-trust and self-confidence. Self-confidence is useful enough, but it is based solely on reason and logic. By its very nature, it leaves out the important emotional and intuitive factors that constitute self-trust. Self-trust may seem to fly in the face of pure reason, but it has a truth of its own that must be heard. Both self-confidence and self-trust are necessary if one is to make effective, viable decisions relating to one's own life.

Trust and no trust

In the two previous chapters, we have already become acquainted with some examples of self-trust, and also with examples of how damaging it can be to lack trust in oneself.

Phil, the young lawyer in Chapter 1, who gave up the idea of working in a big-city law firm and instead sought a low-pressure job in a low-pressure community, is an example of someone who did eventually trust himself. He ignored conventional "wisdom" and listened to his own inner voice that had been trying to tell him what he himself was like and what kind of life he would be comfortable living.

Sam, the computer scientist-consultant, who can never finish his assignments but keeps amassing more and more data, is a prime example of lack of self-trust. He needs to consult his inner self to find out why the role of consultant makes him so uncomfortable and, if necessary, to modify his career to conform to what his instincts are trying to tell him.

Sandy, the woman who discarded a romantic but unreliable lover, did trust herself. She listened to the inner voice conveying her craving for another kind of man and for stability in her life. Sharon, the free-lance writer, also found self-trust. She accepted her need for a solitary, creative occupation and gave up the frustrating pseudo-career of club woman.

In contrast, there was the woman (in Chapter 2) who wanted to go back to work but did not trust her ability to cope with the outside world. Instead, she allowed herself to be intimidated by a husband who deprecated her. She could only have gotten out of her own way by trusting her own sense that she needed to exchange her sterile home life for further education and a more rewarding occupation.

Some people stay in bad marriages, perennially miserable, because they do not trust their own feelings about the unsuitability of the relationship. Many endure unpleasant jobs or the wrong career, refusing to confront their own needs, fearing to trust the impulse to switch to something different. Almost every problem is compounded by failure to listen to (trust) one's own emotions. But emotions have something important to tell you. Cold logic applied to a life equation leaves out an important factor: what your heart has to say.

What used to be called a "courting" situation is a prime example of the mistakes people make in creating their own destiny, when they ignore inner voices and fail to trust themselves. Boy meets girl; woman meets man. They are physically attracted. But they hide from each other and also from themselves major aspects of their true nature. They think: "If he (or she) knew what I'm really like, he (she) might not love me." So they suppress their essential selves and could end up in a destructive semipermanent relationship leading, eventually, to breakup or divorce. Sadly, it is only when such a relationship does collapse, when the ill-mated individual listens to inner needs, that he or she can at last become "self-actualized."

Self-actualized?

Is "self-actualized" some kind of scientific jargon for good old self-indulgence? Not at all. When respected scholar Abraham Maslow coined the term, he was describing the basic urge of any human being "to become everything one is capable of becoming." It is natural for all of us to want to be fully ourselves, to be whatever it is that we are uniquely suited to be or to do. A Gauguin becomes self-actualized by going to the South Seas and painting masterpieces. A stockbroker at age 65, after his wife's death, becomes a Roman Catholic priest. He tells an interviewer: "It may sound corny, but I wanted to have more self-fulfillment. I just wanted a different type of life. I wanted to serve Christ and my fellow man."

Self-indulgence is self-destructive gluttony, pandering to one's selfish desires in any area (not only food), no matter what the cost to the well-being of others or to one's own physical or mental health. In contrast, self-actualization means listening to one's inner self, trusting oneself, and fulfilling the promise of one's peculiar capabilities and talents. A carpenter is self-actualized if he or she loves that kind of work and is eminently suited to do it. But a musician could possibly not be self-actualized if that person's inner need is to do social work instead of following the family's musical tradition. Whatever course one takes, in marriage, in career, in life-style, is right only if that course has been plotted with due regard to both external reality and the truth that resides within one. Trust your deepest impulses: they also represent truth.

A key element

Self-trust turns out to be a key element in almost any life problem: in vocational problems, in problems relating to love and marriage, even in problems having to do with one's ability to learn a new skill or a new subject matter. Self-trust, listening to that sixth sense, should be a compass even in the little things, the trivial as well as the crucial. Take the student who studies every night, like everybody else, and who is involved in a hopeless struggle against an inner time clock that says: "You are at your best in the morning." If he or she trusts that inner self, the obvious solution is to get up at 5 A.M. to study and spend the evenings at the movies or on the beach or playing poker. Other students take copious notes in class. They might do well to heed their urge to listen to the lecture, even enjoy it, and put down important impressions afterward.

Listening to one's inner self even applies to sports. If you hate to jog, why do it? Find some other activity. If you try too hard when you swing the golf club, you are probably missing half your shots. The trouble is that your brain is expecting too much. Your unheeded inner self is telling you to relax and have fun. If you listen and do relax, you'll hit the golf ball better (ask any pro).

Relax. Let come what may. Go with the flow. Don't let your "logical" expectations tense you up and block out good, serendipitous happenings. Madame Curie discovered radium by accident. She might not have recognized her discovery for the remarkable breakthrough that it was, had she been locked into logical expectations.

To learn to trust oneself is more than a technique. It is a way of life useful in all areas, in every period, in good seasons and in bad. Do you have the habit of self-trust now? How do you make important decisions? Do you trust your head? Do you trust your heart? A combination of the two is essential if you are to attain that elusive state we call happiness. How much head and how much heart? The mix is up to you. If you trust yourself you will do it right.

Let us assess your trust level.

Measuring trust

In recent years, much has been written by social scientists about trust. It remained for Dr. Jack R. Gibb to devise an easy-to-use self-diagnosis scale to enable an individual to measure his or her own level of self-trust.* This is a pencil-and-paper exercise that will take only a few minutes to complete. Just fill in the blanks, then add up your score for each of the eight categories.

TORI self-diagnosis scale

Instructions: In front of each of the following items, place the letter that corresponds to your degree of agreement or disagreement with this statement.

SD = strongly disagree D = disagree A = agree SA = strongly agree

_____ 1. I feel that no matter what I might do, people generally would accept and understand me.

_____ 2. I feel that there are large areas of me that I don't share with other people.

_____ 3. I usually assert myself in most situations in life.

_____ 4. I seldom seek help from others.

_____ 5. Most people tend to trust each other.

_____ 6. People are usually not interested in what others say.

_____ 7. Most people exert little pressure on other people to try to get them to do what they should be doing.

_____ 8. Most people do their own thing with little thought for others.

_____ 9. I feel that I am usually a very cautious person.

_____ 10. I feel little need to cover up the things I do and keep them from others.

_____ 11. I usually try to do what I'm supposed to be doing.

*Reproduced from John E. Jones and J. William Pfeiffer, eds., *The 1977 Annual Handbook for Group Facilitators* (La Jolla, California: University Associates, 1977). Used with permission.

_____ 12. I find that people are usually willing to help me when I want help or ask for it.

_____ 13. Most people in life are more interested in getting things done than in caring for each other as individuals.

_____ 14. Most people usually tell it like it is.

_____ 15. Most people do what they ought to do in life, out of a sense of responsibility to others.

_____ 16. Most people that I meet "have it together" at a fairly deep level.

_____ 17. I usually trust the people I meet.

_____ 18. I am afraid that if I showed my real innermost thoughts to most people, they would be shocked.

_____ 19. In most life situations I feel free to do what I want to do.

_____ 20. I often feel that I am a minority in the groups I belong to.

_____ 21. People that I meet usually seem to know who they are; they have a real sense of being individuals.

_____ 22. Most people I know and work with are very careful to express only relevant and appropriate ideas when we do things together.

_____ 23. Most people's goals are very clear to them and they know what they are doing in life.

_____ 24. Most groups I work with or live in have a hard time getting together and doing something they have decided to do.

_____ 25. If I left most groups I belong to, they would miss me very little.

_____ 26. I can trust most people I know with my most private and significant feelings and opinions.

_____ 27. I find that my goals are different from the goals of most people I work with.

_____ 28. I look forward to getting together with the people in the groups I belong to.

_____ 29. Most persons I meet are playing roles and not being themselves.

_____ 30. Most of the people I know communicate with each other very well.

_____ 31. In most of the groups I belong to members put pressure on each other toward group goals.

_____ 32. In an emergency most people act in caring and effective ways.

_____ 33. I almost always feel very good about myself as a person.

_____ 34. If I have negative feelings I do not express them easily.

_____ 35. It is easy for me to take risks in my life.

_____ 36. I often go along with others simply because I feel a sense of obligation to do what is expected.

_____ 37. People in the groups I belong to seem to care very much for each other as individuals.

_____ 38. Most people tend to be dishonest.

_____ 39. Most people I know let others be where they are and how they are.

_____ 40. Most people like either to lead or to be led, rather than to work together with others as equals.

_____ 41. My relationships with most people are impersonal.

_____ 42. Whenever I feel strongly about something I feel comfortable expressing myself to others.

_____ 43. I feel that I have to keep myself under wraps in most life situations.

_____ 44. I usually enjoy working with people.

_____ 45. Most people I know seem to play definite and clear roles and to be respected on the basis of how well they perform the roles.

_____ 46. When the people I know have negative feelings they usually express them at some point.

_____ 47. A large portion of the people in groups I belong to are very apathetic and passive.

_____ 48. Most of the people I am usually with are well integrated at many levels.

_____ 49. I feel like a unique person and I like being unique.

_____ 50. I would feel very vulnerable if I told most people I know my most secret and private feelings and opinions.

_____ 51. Most of the people I know feel that my personal growth is important.

_____ 52. I often don't feel like cooperating with others.

_____ 53. People usually have a high opinion of my contributions to the groups I'm in and the conversations I have.

_____ 54. Most people are afraid to be open and honest with others.

_____ 55. The people that I know usually express what they want pretty well.

_____ 56. Most people are pretty individualistic and do not work together well as members of a team.

_____ 57. I often don't feel very good about myself.

_____ 58. I usually feel free to be exactly who I am and not to pretend I am something else.

_____ 59. I feel that it is important in life to make a reasonable attempt to meet others' expectations of me.

_____ 60. I feel a sense of interconnectedness with the people I associate with and would miss anyone who left my circle of friends and associates.

_____ 61. It is easy to tell who the "in" people are in the groups I associate with.

_____ 62. Most people listen to others with understanding and empathy.

_____ 63. It seems to me that a great many people spend energy trying to get others to do things they don't really want to do.

_____ 64. I think that most people I know enjoy being with people.

_____ 65. The groups that I associate with see me as an important group member.

_____ 66. My ideas and opinions are often distorted by others.

_____ 67. My basic goals in life are similar to the basic goals of other people.

_____ 68. People are seldom willing to give me help on the things that really matter to me.

_____ 69. People usually listen to the things that I say.

_____ 70. It seems to me that when they feel negative most people keep it to themselves.

_____ 71. The groups that I'm associated with usually have a lot of energy that gets directed into whatever the group does.

_____ 72. You really have to have some power if you want to get anything done in this life.

_____ 73. I often don't feel very genuine and real when I'm with people.

_____ 74. There is very little I don't know about the friends that I associate closely with.

_____ 75. If I did what I really wanted to do in life, I would be doing different things from what I am now doing.

_____ 76. I am often aware of how other people help me in what I am trying to do in life.

_____ 77. It seems to me that most people live in fear.

_____ 78. The people I know are usually very spontaneous and uninhibited with each other.

_____ 79. Most people are very unclear about what they want out of life.

_____ 80. Most of the groups I work with or live in have good team or cooperative relationships.

_____ 81. I care very much for the people I associate with.

_____ 82. People often misunderstand me and how I feel.

_____ 83. When I am with others and we reach a decision about something we want to do I am usually in complete agreement with what we have decided.

_____ 84. I have no real sense of belonging to the groups I associate with.

_____ 85. In the groups I belong to, people treat others as important and significant people.

_____ 86. It is easy for me to express positive feelings, but very difficult for me to express negative feelings to others.

_____ 87. Most of the people I know are growing and changing all the time.

_____ 88. It seems to me that most people need a lot of controls to keep them on the right track.

_____ 89. I often feel defensive.

_____ 90. I keep very few secrets from my associates.

_____ 91. It is often not OK for me to be myself in the groups I'm in.

_____ 92. I feel a strong sense of belonging to several groups in my life.

_____ 93. In the groups I belong to it is easy to see who is important and who is unimportant.

_____ 94. Most people don't keep a lot of secrets from others.

_____ 95. In the groups I belong to a lot of our energy goes into irrelevant and unimportant things.

_____ 96. It seems to me that there is very little destructive competition among the people I know and associate with.

TORI self-diagnosis scale score sheet

Instructions: The TORI Self-Diagnosis Scale yields eight scores: four depicting how you see yourself in your life in terms of the four core growth processes (Trusting-being; Opening; Realizing-becoming; and Interdepending), and four capturing your sense of what the people and world around you are like. Look back at the items for one of the eight scales on the instrument to see how you responded. On the Score Sheet, circle your response for each item according to whether you marked "Strongly Disagree," "Disagree ," etc. Then sum the item scores for the scale. Do the same for each scale.

Trusting-being

Item Score				
Item	SD	D	A	SA
1.	0	1	2	3
9.	3	2	1	0
17.	0	1	2	3
25.	3	2	1	0
33.	0	1	2	3
41.	3	2	1	0
49.	0	1	2	3
57.	3	2	1	0
65.	0	1	2	3
73.	3	2	1	0
81.	0	1	2	3
89.	3	2	1	0

Opening-showing

Item Score				
Item	SD	D	A	SA
2.	3	2	1	0
10.	0	1	2	3
18.	3	2	1	0
26.	0	1	2	3
34.	3	2	1	0
42.	0	1	2	3
50.	3	2	1	0
58.	0	1	2	3
66.	3	2	1	0
74.	0	1	2	3
82.	3	2	1	0
90.	0	1	2	3

Realizing-becoming

Item Score				
Item	SD	D	A	SA
3.	0	1	2	3
11.	3	2	1	0
19.	0	1	2	3
27.	3	2	1	0
35.	0	1	2	3
43.	3	2	1	0
51.	0	1	2	3
59.	3	2	1	0
67.	0	1	2	3
75.	3	2	1	0
83.	0	1	2	3
91.	3	2	1	0

Interdepending-interbeing

Item Score				
Item	SD	D	A	SA
4.	3	2	1	0
12.	0	1	2	3
20.	3	2	1	0
28.	0	1	2	3
36.	3	2	1	0
44.	0	1	2	3
52.	3	2	1	0
60.	0	1	2	3
68.	3	2	1	0
76.	0	1	2	3
84.	3	2	1	0
92.	0	1	2	3

How I see *Myself* in life

T ☐   O ☐   R ☐   I ☐

Trusting-being

Item Score

Item	SD	D	A	SA
5.	0	1	2	3
13.	3	2	1	0
21.	0	1	2	3
29.	3	2	1	0
37.	0	1	2	3
45.	3	2	1	0
53.	0	1	2	3
61.	3	2	1	0
69.	0	1	2	3
77.	3	2	1	0
85.	0	1	2	3
93.	3	2	1	0

Opening-showing

Item Score

Item	SD	D	A	SA
6.	3	2	1	0
14.	0	1	2	3
22.	3	2	1	0
30.	0	1	2	3
38.	3	2	1	0
46.	0	1	2	3
54.	3	2	1	0
62.	0	1	2	3
70.	3	2	1	0
78.	0	1	2	3
86.	3	2	1	0
94.	0	1	2	3

Realizing-becoming

Item Score

Item	SD	D	A	SA
7.	0	1	2	3
15.	3	2	1	0
23.	0	1	2	3
31.	3	2	1	0
39.	0	1	2	3
47.	3	2	1	0
55.	0	1	2	3
63.	3	2	1	0
71.	0	1	2	3
79.	3	2	1	0
87.	0	1	2	3
95.	3	2	1	0

Interdepending-interbeing

Item Score

Item	SD	D	A	SA
8.	3	2	1	0
16.	0	1	2	3
24.	3	2	1	0
32.	0	1	2	3
40.	3	2	1	0
48.	0	1	2	3
56.	3	2	1	0
64.	0	1	2	3
72.	3	2	1	0
80.	0	1	2	3
88.	3	2	1	0
96.	0	1	2	3

How I see the People World

T ☐   O ☐   R ☐   I ☐

What does all this mean? According to Gibb, trust has eight different aspects. The first four relate to one's trust-related attitudes toward oneself. The second four relate to one's trust-related attitudes toward people and the world around one.

Now you can assess your own level of trust in each of these eight areas. Note that a high score in any area ranges from 24 to 36. A low score may be considered anything from 0 to 12. Here is Gibb's analysis of what your scores mean with regard to trust.

Interpretation sheet TORI self-diagnosis scale

Trusting-being:

A person who scores *high* on this set of items is saying:

View of Myself: "I trust myself, have a fairly well-formed sense of my own being and uniqueness, and feel good about myself as a person."

View of People: "I tend to see people as trusting, and as providing a good environment for me to live and be in."

A person who scores *low* on this set of items is saying:

View of Myself: "I feel less trusting of myself, have a less well-formed sense of my own being and uniqueness, and feel less well about myself as a person."

View of People: "I tend to see people as un-trusting, as impersonal and in role, and as providing a somewhat threatening and defense-producing environment for me and for others.

Opening-showing:

A person who scores *high* on this set of items is saying:

View of Myself: "I feel free to show myself to others, show who I am, and express my feelings and attitudes with little pretense or cover-up."

View of People: "I tend to see people as open and spontaneous and as willing to show themselves to each other."

A person who scores *low* on this set of items is saying:

View of Myself: "I feel un-free to be open, feel vulnerable and un-safe, and I think it is necessary to keep large areas of myself private and unshared."

View of People: "I tend to see people as fearful, cautious, and unwilling to show feelings and opinions, particularly those feelings and opinions that are negative or non-supportive."

Realizing-becoming

A person who scores *high* on this set of items is saying:

View of Myself: "I feel free to take risks, assert myself, do anything that I really want to do, and follow my intrinsic motivations. I have a sense of self-realization."

View of People: "I tend to see people as allowing others their freedom, and as providing an environment for me and others that nourishes our striving for intrinsic goals. People allow others to be who they are."

A person who scores *low* on this set of items is saying:

View of Myself: "I am aware of the pressure of extrinsic motivations. I feel that I must try to do what I am supposed to do and that I must attempt to meet the expectations of others."

View of People: "I tend to see other people as exerting pressures on me and others to conform, to do things that we may not want to do, and to work towards goals that are not significant to me as a person."

Interdepending-interbeing:

A person who scores *high* on this set of items is saying:

View of Myself: "I have a strong sense of belonging to the groups that are important to me, and I enjoy working with, helping, or meeting with other people."

View of People: "I tend to see other people as cooperative, working effectively, and relatively well integrated into the life around them and the groups they belong to."

A person who scores *low* on this set of items is saying:

View of Myself: "I do not have a strong sense of belonging to the groups of which I am a member, and do not especially enjoy working with others in a team way. I have competitive, dependent, or other feelings that get in the way of my teaming with others."

View of People: "I tend to see other people as not being cooperative and not working well with others. I see people in general as not easy to work with or team with and as having feelings that get in their way."

Do you have some idea now of how much you trust yourself? Are you surprised? The chances are that your trust level is too low for comfort, that is, lower than it should be if you are to help yourself to get out of your own way in solving the problems of your life. But do not despair. There are ways of getting in touch with one's inner self (selves) and developing trust in those internal friends with whom we all are blessed.

A journey

Would you like to tap your own inner wisdom? Are you in a mood to trust what you find within your consciousness? Remember that trust is the basis of all relationships, with oneself as well as with others. Without trust, any relationship is superficial and unrewarding. If you cannot let yourself heed your own instincts, if you cannot permit yourself to pay attention to what is really bothering you, then you will never solve the problems of your life. You can be your own "doctor," but only if you put yourself in that physician's hands. Give the doctor your trust and listen to the diagnosis. The right prescription will follow.

Are you ready to take a journey to meet your Inner Wisdom figure?

First, choose a time and a place where you can be alone with yourself and be comfortable. Select your favorite chair. Or perhaps it is a couch or a bed, a lounge chair on the lawn or a drifting rowboat. Choose a time when you will be uninterrupted. Morning? Evening? Afternoon? It doesn't matter, except to you.

Insulate yourself from competitive sound, unless it makes you relax to have soft music in the background. A ticking clock in the room (if you are indoors) is a good idea, if you have such an old-fashioned timepiece. But the clock is not essential. All that matters is a relaxed, comfortable atmosphere, no interruptions, and your own desire to take a trip to meet the Wizard.

Where do you want to go? Do you want to hike with a picnic basket up to a mountaintop where you can see the view in every direction? Do you choose to drive to a lakeshore where the sunshine is dappled by big trees and the surface of the water is disturbed only by occasional insects? Is a quiet stretch of beach by the ocean your destination? Or the old-fashioned porch of a farmhouse in the country? Or a terrace 30 stories above the city streets? Or a quiet room in a resort hotel? Wherever you choose to go is right, if it will make you happy and relaxed.

Prepare for the journey. Relax and start to count, slowly, to 20. Let your eyes close now, or soon, whenever that feels comfortable to you. Between numbers, tell yourself how comfortable and relaxed you feel. Put aside the outside world. Breathe very deeply. Get into a semi-waking state. You are beginning to breathe more and more deeply, feeling more comfortable with each breath. You are relaxing more and more. You are feeling the chair or the bed supporting you, and you are luxuriating in the feeling of being cradled. When you finally reach the count of 20, open your eyes and start your trip to your chosen place. Imagine the preparations. Imagine the drive or the hike. Imagine your happy approach to the designated spot. Glory in the view when you get there, in the peace and solitude, in the beauty, in the happy memories or expectations that the place arouses.

Now look over your shoulder to the middle distance. A figure is approaching you. It is indistinct. Man? Woman? The figure is hazy but it is near you, waiting expectantly. Have you a question? What has been bothering you before you came on this trip? Would you like to ask this wise person about it? Would you like to talk it over? Have a conversation. This is a friend, a wise friend, someone you can trust implicitly.

Talk it all over, whatever has been bothering you. Whatever this wise person tells you: accept! This is your own inner truth. Converse as long as you like. And when the conversation is over, thank your companion, and say good-bye, knowing in your heart that you can call on this same wise friend any time you wish. Now count from 20 to 1 and come back thoughtfully to where you began.

Does it work?

Are you skeptical about the process? Do you feel a bit foolish about undertaking such a journey? Do you doubt the existence of the wise figure whom we call Inner Wisdom? Perhaps a true story of one who went on such a journey, who also began with skepticism, will convince you.

This woman—let us call her C.—had been suffering from stomach pains, nothing violent, but enough to worry her. Could it be cancer? Could it be the beginning of heart trouble? She had seen a doctor who could find nothing seriously wrong with her, though "at your age" it might have been something significant. "Watch your diet," C. was told, "and report back if the symptoms persist." The symptoms ebbed and waned, then came back. C. came to the conclusion that she might have some other problem. But what?

Not believing, resisting a little, nevertheless she agreed to take the Inner Wisdom journey. She chose as her destination a mountaintop in Hawaii she had once visited on vacation. Trudging up the mountain gave her great pleasure, as she anticipated the beauty of the view. But she realized when she got to the top that she was not alone, in spite of the instructions that this was to be a solitary expedition. Her husband was there; it was he who was the shadowy figure. She could not utter her problem to him. But she did not need to say anything. Aware of her husband's wordless presence, and her inability to keep him out of her imaginary trip, she realized what was the cause of her stomachaches. Trusting the vision, she became aware that she had retreated into hypochrondria, a more acceptable "rational" fear than her fear of losing her husband, of being left alone in the world. The fear of his death was connected not only to her physical discomfort but also to the mild depression she had been experiencing off and on for a long time.

"What if I lost him? I cannot manage by myself!" she told the figure on the mountaintop. And the figure replied: "Nonsense! You can cope with anything that happens. You have many resources. You are smart, strong, sturdy. Your husband's death would be a tragic loss, but in due time you would be able to go on by yourself. Think of the friends you have—many are *your* friends, not his. Think of the skills you have— yours, not his. Think of the special interests in your life—yours, not his. Think of the trips you might take, trips in which he has never been interested. There could, conceivably, be other men who would eventually interest you. Why not? You're not so hideous. You're even presentable. You're smart. You will figure it out and you will go on living if you have to!"

Mysteriously, she felt comforted. It was all true, she realized. She would cope. She could trust herself. She had an enormous feeling of relief. It was time to come down the mountain and go home.

C., who had been skeptical, was now home again, back in the quiet room with the ticking clock. She indulged in a quiet smile. She acknowledged to herself the fear, the legitimate fear, that in the course of time she might be left a widow. That foreboding had poisoned her soul as well as her body. Till this moment, she had not trusted herself to confront the problem of her own and her husband's mortality. But now she was beginning to believe that maybe she did have the inner wherewithal to cope, when and if the worst came to pass.

Like C., you must trust yourself and trust the process. What have you learned about yourself? Self-trust is the first step in utilizing your own resources so that you can achieve self-fulfillment. The next step is "owning."

4

Owning

JANE W. IS HAVING TROUBLE changing jobs. She "freezes" in interviews. "I don't like to brag," she confessed to the counselor whom she consulted out of desperation. Evidently, she had been taught early in her life that "it's not nice to toot your own horn." So now she cannot accept her own superior qualifications by uttering them out loud.

Frederick I., a man who is seriously overweight, only looks at his face in the mirror. "I don't look so bad," he reassures himself. "Only a couple of pounds less would do it." Therefore he allows himself to order the chocolate mousse for dessert.

Linda is an alcoholic. But that term has never crossed her mind. "Occasionally, I have a little too much," she tells herself. "But I can take it or leave it." Unfortunately, leaving her is what her husband is thinking about.

In conversation, John is always bringing up the problem of the large number of homosexuals in San Francisco, where he lives. He is terribly worried about the situation, he tells acquaintances. But the marriage counselor who is trying to help John and his wife has noted a serious problem area. John, the therapist has surmised, has a strange attitude toward his wife. Could he have homosexual tendencies?

These are only a few examples of people who are getting in their own way by failing to own their own characteristics. Like the fat man, they cannot bring themselves to look in a full-length mirror. And thus they are ignoring qualities that are hindering them, or qualities that could help them lead a more fulfilling, happier life. Most of us share this common problem: we do not "own" ourselves completely.

Renter or owner?

Have you ever rented a house or apartment? No sense painting it yourself, or moving a wall for better space arrangement, or changing the light fixtures. After all, it's not your place. Why make improvements? So you continue to live in the place, at least for a while, just half satisfied. Not too serious, perhaps, though uncomfortable. But we occupy our bodies and our souls throughout our lives. How wasteful, to rent and to make no necessary adjustments, to take insufficient advantage of what we are! Why not own?

A recent *New York Times* feature story told about several people who, in contrast to Jane and Frederick and Linda and John, had accepted themselves. The story didn't mention "owning" but that is what it was all about. The article spoke glowingly about the changes these people had been able to make in their own lives.

One man in his forties gave up teaching and began to do carpentry and odd jobs in order to have more time to study painting. A young woman who had an impressive job in the White House resigned and opened a catering business and grocery store. Why? "My job in Washington was intellectually exciting and stimulating but it wasn't me at all."

An interior decorator making big money gave it up to open a store selling used but elegant clothes and accessories. The new business yielded meager returns but he is now "much happier."

Owning—facing up to one's own characteristics, emotions, fears, weaknesses, strengths—is something that few of us do completely. And yet it is not possible to live a truly fulfilled life until we recognize, accept, and let others know who we are and what we are and what we realistically could be.

True, it can be very frightening to look deep into oneself and accept what has been half-hidden all these years. Who wants to admit to him or herself, or to let the world know, that "I am an alcoholic, I have a serious drinking problem"? And yet no cure can be undertaken unless the alcoholic does make such an admission.

It is not easy to accept the need to exchange a prestigious job for low-status blue-collar work, even though contentment may be impossible in the former and a real probability in the latter.

Terror prevents a conventionally minded latent homosexual from facing that tendency. And yet a heterosexual marriage is in shambles because reality has not been dealt with.

It is certainly discomforting to look at the wrinkles that denote advancing age and to accept the implications. Equally threatening is the view of the fat man in the full-length mirror. Nevertheless, ultimate happiness comes from awareness, owning, and taking responsibility for *everything* that one is: good, bad, indifferent, or just plain different.

To own oneself at last is to acquire the ability to set one's sights on a better way of life. Failing to own oneself is to play a card game without a full deck. Bad enough to be cheated by the dealer, but much worse to cheat oneself.

Have you completely owned yourself? Are you entirely aware of who and what you are? Are you living under an assumed name? Would you like to find out?

See yourself in others

Strangely enough, an excellent mirror in which to see yourself is someone who has some characteristics that get under your skin.

Everybody knows such people, not only acquaintances but also close friends and relatives. These people sometimes behave or think in a manner that drives you up a wall. You find in them traits you can't abide. It could be dishonesty. Or excessive materialism. Or loud, boastful behavior. Or sexual infidelity. Or vulgarity. These are only a few examples.

But an equally useful mirror is a person you admire. A successful businessman. A beautiful woman. An individual who speaks well. A compassionate, selfless soul. An outgoing life-of-the-party.

Not everybody admires the same kinds of people. And not everybody is irritated by the same traits in others. Our tastes in people vary enormously. But they are significant because in others we see ourselves.

For example: A man who has three sons is constantly at odds only with the eldest. These clashes started in the boy's babyhood and continued into his early adulthood. Then the relationship improved and eventually the two became the best of friends. The significance of this stormy and then amicable relationship escaped both father and son. But the wife and mother, who knew them both exceedingly well, understood what was happening. The father fought with the characteristics in his son which were, in fact, his own characteristics. But as the youth mellowed into adulthood, the father and son became a mutual admiration society. Now they saw in each other mirror images and they liked what they saw. Nevertheless, when disagreements arose between the two adults (father and son) the clash usually revolved around idiosyncrasies the two shared. Unfortunately, neither one looked into the mirror that revealed them both. The mother and wife, confidante of both men, tried to tell each of them that he was fighting with his own self, failing to own his own traits and tendencies. (Of course, they didn't listen.)

What is the significance of this father-son vignette? It is applicable to everybody. In your case, it may not be your son or daughter or father or mother who rouses you to anger, irritation, or admiration. But whoever excites in you negative or positive feelings has something to tell you about yourself.

For example, of all the characteristics in your friend, why is her excessive materialism the one trait that irritates you? The answer is simple, if you will only own it: you, yourself, are also somewhat materialistic but you have disowned that part of yourself. Somewhere you learned that love of clothes and jewelry and big cars is "not nice." So you stuffed that tendency out of sight, deep in your unconscious. It comes out only as self-righteous annoyance with a good friend. But if you accept the truth about yourself, you will at the very least feel better about your friend. And you might be better able to enjoy your own extravagant purchase that was spoiled because you felt guilty.

In the traits you admire in others are also clues to your own tendencies, characteristics that you have suppressed, failed to own—at a real loss to yourself. A woman in your social group is outgoing, warm, friendly, and gets along with everybody. You, who sit silent, both admire and envy her. Stop and think! What's keeping you from coming out of your shell? Is it a parent's admonition long ago that children should be seen and not heard? Did a teacher put you down for talking in class? Where did you get the idea that you are only a listener? Own your suppressed social self! In you is a latent life of the party, just like the woman you admire.

Think about the characteristics of one or two people you wish you could be like. Think about the characteristics of one or two people who bother you. Jot down, if you like, a list of those characteristics. Can you honestly say you can't find your secret self in all of them? Own what you find. It could come in handy.

Boasting

Another way to find yourself and set yourself on the road to full ownership of what you possess is to play the boasting game. This takes courage because it requires you to behave in a way that mother taught you never to do. You must be a braggart. Saying it to yourself doesn't count.

For the boasting exercise to work you must find a partner whom you trust and who is willing to put him/herself on the line also. Choose a close friend. Your mate. Your mother or father. Select anyone you trust, anyone who can be made to understand that you are working on a courageous and important project: owning yourself and thus helping yourself to understand You. Point out, if necessary, that the exercise will be useful to your friend, too. (Who in this world scorns a bit of self-improvement?)

The boasting game should be played in privacy. Take a walk together, have lunch, sit down over a soft drink or a cup of coffee. Agree that for the next half hour or so you will repeal all the conventional prohibitions about tooting one's own horn. You will, by mutual agreement, be blatantly frank about how good you are. You will assign yourselves each to find four areas in which you will confess, out loud, your achievement and superiority. No head bowed, no eyes averted. You will say it in words and without hesitation, doubt, or false modesty. Both of you will do it. That will make it even and thus nobody will be embarrassed.

You will be surprised at the outcome.

Want a preview?

A dialogue

Here is part of a boasting dialogue shared with the authors by a husband and wife. The wife was trying to deal with some nagging frustrations and she asked her husband to go along with her efforts. He was reluctant, because he was not one for introspection, but he agreed because he knew how much this effort meant to her.

She   (taking a deep breath and plunging in): I am very well organized. In fact, I think I am an excellent manager. I manage the house. I manage you. I manage the children. I could really manage anything.

He   (being fair): That's true. You are very well organized. Of course, so am I.

She   (surprising herself): In fact, I could run an office! Now that's a job I could do. It's no different from what I've been doing for years. Being organized is being organized. Do you think I could get a job like that? (laughs deprecatingly).

He   Why not? If you really want . . .

She   (interrupting): I really *could* manage an office. But who would believe me? Of course (musing) I could try to talk myself into a job. Would I have the nerve . . . Well, I could just talk my way in. I really am a good manager. And I certainly know how to talk—at home. I'm being honest about all this. If . . .

He   (interrupting): Honesty. That's *my* strength. But it strikes me that it's a liability, too. I guess I really do go overboard. It must be because I'm so afraid to giving in to any impulse to be dishonest . . .

She   You, dishonest? You're my example of an honesty nut!

He   Of course I could be dishonest! If I let myself. I have to fight with myself . . .

She   You do, really?

He   Of course, did you think I was some kind of saint? Everybody has a streak of dishonesty.

She   We never talked about this before. You always acted so sure of yourself. I never dreamed. . . .

The conversation lasted for two hours. In the course of it, this couple uncovered information about themselves and each other that was new and different and thought-provoking. Both realized that they had stumbled on exciting truths. One practical outcome for the wife was finding a talent she had previously ignored: her ability to manage. Till then, she had devalued her accomplishments as something any housewife could do. Now, having recognized and owned this asset, she could even consider turning it into a paying job. And she found, too, that now she had the latent self-confidence to go out and sell herself to an employer.

As for the husband, for the first time he consciously recognized and owned the duality in his own nature. His squeaky-clean image of himself changed to a more realistic acceptance of the weaknesses he shared with all humanity. It was a relief to him to get off his pedestal. (His wife was somewhat relieved, too.)

This is not a made-up example. It illustrates how useful it can be at last to take a good look at your own strengths and weaknesses, previously hidden from yourself and probably from the world. Like this woman who suddenly realized new uses for her managerial ability, you may find that giving voice to your own abilities can suggest exciting new possibilities for putting them to work. And like the man who confronted his own excessive rectitude and thus became aware that he feared his hidden dishonesty, you may find it can be a relief to reduce tension by realizing that you share frailties with the rest of humankind. By turning on the light and getting a good look at our fears, we usually find them to be harmless figments of our imagination.

Going public

Coming out of the closet by boasting to one trusted companion leads to another important step in self-confrontation. It is now less threatening to go public with others as well. Most of us hide behind an assumed identity, thus erecting an invisible wall between us and everybody else. But in tearing down that wall, revealing ourselves to others, we reveal ourselves to ourselves. And the horrid feeling of going about the world incognito is replaced by a heady sense of liberation.

Think how much tension you accumulate when you deal with other people while wearing your customary disguise. For instance, you play the part of a conscientious mother of teenagers, faithfully carpooling and admonishing and setting an example—but inside you still lives the young girl who likes to dance and party. Or—you go forth each day in your suit and tie, sit at a desk, issue orders to subordinates, and agree soberly with a superior who issues orders to you. But by the time evening comes it is not only the tie that you ache to remove but also that constricted personality who sat behind the desk.

Whatever the role you play, you are undoubtedly sending false messages about who and what you are, not only to the world but also to yourself. Wouldn't it be a relief to relax and be yourself for a change?

The way to do it is, first, to play the boasting game with an intimate. Then, second, be yourself (as you now surmise your real self to be), in a public situation.

There are several different ways to go public. For example, an out-of-control drinker goes to Alcoholics Anonymous and makes that important announcement to all who are present: "I am an alcoholic." A young woman has coffee with her suburban neighbors and dares to talk about what she has previously concealed (for fear of rejection): that she has a Ph.D. in history. A homosexual goes out for a drink with coworkers and comes out of the closet (to the relief of everyone who has guessed already). A man who has for years sat on beaches and looked longingly at sailboats actually buys one.

Going public will benefit you in more ways than one. If you dare to be yourself at last, you will almost certainly discover that your social life has suddenly and dramatically improved. Human contacts prosper only if people are allowed to know who you are. Going public can lead us to new friendships, new loves, and even new jobs. Very likely people won't even act surprised when you reveal your undisguised self. They will probably feel relieved by the withdrawal of tension between you and everybody else. Whatever your newly revealed persona—intellectual, playgirl/boy, alcoholic, Cadillac-lover—they suspected it all along. And even if they didn't, they're delighted and fascinated by the new You.

And you, too, will feel delighted and relieved. Allowing yourself to come out of that self-imposed shell is as easeful as taking off tight shoes. Unless you happen to be a professional actor who is used to playing a role, your emergence as yourself at last will give you undreamed-of comfort. Let it all hang out. What bliss!

Finally, you will achieve the ultimate benefit of going public. Accepting your own reality will make it possible for you to change that reality, if change now seems desirable. Once you have let the world know who you are, you will feel free to work toward modifying those aspects of yourself that are troublesome. For instance, if you are an alcoholic, you can now work at controlling alcoholism, unconstrained by the necessity of hiding your weakness from yourself and from the world. If you gave in to your enthusiasm about sailboats, once you have gotten that out of your system you might decide you don't like sailboats so much after all. If you're the housewife with the Ph.D., having discovered that your neighbors were not at all troubled by finding out that you are "different," you might openly consider the possibility of getting a babysitter for your children and a job to match your Ph.D. As a fat person who can now talk about it, it is now easier to work on becoming a thinner person.

Taking responsibility

All this, of course, is more easily said than done. Going public implies taking responsibility for one's characteristics and then, inevitably, doing something constructive about who and what you are. But there are built-in obstacles.

One is fear.

"How can I become talkative and lively at the party when everyone knows I'm the quiet one? I'm afraid they'll laugh at me."

Another obstacle to taking responsibility is a conflict in one's own values.

"How can I possibly date that cute blonde I see every day in the coffee shop? I'm a married man. It's wrong!"

Perhaps even more devastating is low self-esteem, an unconscious conviction that one is incompetent, inept, just not able to cope with the risks that are involved in making changes in one's life.

Are these obstacles preventing you from taking necessary risks to improve your life? If so, can you learn to leap over these personal barriers? Let us explore your predicament in the next chapter.

5

Taking
Risks

A FATHER ARRIVED at the summer camp just as his son was in the midst of a lively basketball game.

"Shoot, Dave!" teammates were yelling. But the boy passed the ball to another. Soon Dave had the ball again.

"Shoot, Dave!" someone shouted. Again he passed the ball.

When the game was over, the father quietly sought out the counselor. "Is Dave a bad shot?" he asked.

"Not at all, he's a good shot," the counselor replied.

"Then why . . . ?"

"I guess he's just afraid he'll miss the basket."

Dave, a teenager, already typifies a problem that keeps adults from getting the most out of their lives. Many of us are afraid to take a shot at what we want. In an earlier chapter, we mentioned the well-qualified consultant who could not bring himself to finish a report, afraid to risk the possibility of leaving something out. A salesman can't seem to close a deal: he cannot risk the turndown. An able employee dares not risk applying for a higher-level position, for fear someone will bring up the fact that she never finished college. Many a teacher gives lecture-only courses, discouraging questions — afraid to risk a query he or she cannot answer.

And yet taking risks is the single most important factor in personal growth. Making a necessary change in one's situation is the only way to improve the quality of life. To risk a move to a new neighborhood. To take steps to change jobs. To speak up in a meeting. To discuss deficiencies in sexual relationships with one's spouse. To take that trip alone. To get a consultation with a makeup expert and change one's face. To break up a destructive personal relationship.

If you are getting in your own way, you undoubtedly need to make a change — to *risk* changes — in your life. How can you get rid of inhibitions against taking risks? What can you do to improve your life? What's stopping you?

Fear of self

The greatest obstacle to taking responsibility and taking necessary risks is the fear of one's own self. An astonishing number of people have a deep-down feeling that they don't measure up. Their self-esteem is low. Their self-image is poor. They dare not risk trusting this inferior creature with important actions and vital decisions.

People with a low regard for themselves see themselves as not really able to meet some vague standard of which they themselves are only half-conscious. Perhaps they are responding to early training by overly conscientious parents.

A child is often taught that he or she is incompetent.

"Don't touch that—you'll break it." "Don't handle that tool—you'll hurt yourself." "Don't cross the street—you'll get run over." "Mother knows best." "Father knows best."

The child grows up to be a man or woman, but within, there continues to reside an incompetent bumbler, incapable of making decisions, apt to behave foolishly in public, responding still to "Children should speak when they are spoken to, should be seen but not heard." "What will other people think?" remains the watchword for the not-really-grown-up former child.

In infancy and childhood, we learned not only that mother and father know best but also that mother and father *are* the best. How can one risk knowing more than one's parent, or becoming more competent than one's parent? Freud traced many adult troubles to a basic fear of challenging the supremacy of one's parents. To risk exceeding a parent's success may seem, symbolically, like murdering that parent, even equivalent to incestuously rivaling father or mother for the favors of the opposite-sex parent. What a no-no! What a risk!

Without carrying the Freudian interpretation too far, almost all psychologists credit early training with creating many of the spiritual characteristics of the grown-up child. And yet really to grow up, to take the risks inherent in living an adult life, we must consciously work at throwing off some of the inhibitions built into us during our formative years.

Why don't we?

Habit: safeguard or straitjacket?

Habit, the mindless pseudo-comfort of the familiar, often turns out to be the straitjacket that is keeping us from risking constructive change in our lives. Habit is all that keeps some marriages together. Habit is the glue that binds many people to an unrewarding job. Habit causes a student to keep on frantically taking notes in class, thereby missing the main points of the lecture, instead of using a tape recorder and taking notes later, thoughtfully and selectively. Habit binds us to the same doctor, even though we strongly suspect he is less than competent. Habit permeates our lives.

True, habit is essential. Habit makes it possible to live through each 24 hours without having to make endless exhausting decisions about the routine conduct of our daily round. But some habits could be, in fact, destructive to our ultimate well-being. We cling to the familiar—and thus we box ourselves in.

Please like me!

Taking the risks necessary to improve our lives is impeded by another important barrier: we fear the loss of love and/or social approval. Many a woman in the 1950s and 1960s married and gave up personal abilities, training, talents, and independence, because society expected her to stay home and tend to husband and children full-time. Living that way, many were unhappy, bored, and restless, but dared not risk a change in life-style for fear of the disapproval of husband and everyone else.

Today, the opposite sometimes happens. A woman fears other people's scorn if she chooses to be "only a housewife," even though she may be a born mother and homemaker, a veritable domestic artist.

Do you fear to confront the boss with a legitimate complaint? He might not like you! Are you afraid to state an unpopular opinion at a meeting or in a social group? "They" might disapprove. You're a supervisor: do you hate to fire an incompetent? That person could then be angry at you. You're a professor: is it hard to give a student a well-deserved failing grade? Do you hate to speak up in public because you might make a fool of yourself in front of all those people?

It all comes down to "they might not love/like me!" What price social approval!

A clash of values

Another serious stumbling block in the path of change is a clash in your own values. You are really of two minds about an important situation in your life. Your inner self makes one demand. Your outer self has an opposite priority.

If you are involved in an unsatisfactory personal relationship, one of your selves may want the social security of having a "permanent" lover/wife/husband—but the other you yearns for freedom and more self-expression. A middle-aged woman lavishes endless hours of attention on a demanding, elderly father, to fulfill her self-image as a dutiful, loving daughter who owes her parent whatever the parent chooses to ask of her. But within that adult daughter clamors a rebellious individual who wants desperately to get away, take a trip, have some fun for a change.

Incompatible values pervade almost everyone's life. The chain-smoker values his health, but also values the oral satisfaction and momentary release from tension provided by the act of dragging on the cigarette or sucking on the stem of the pipe. The conscientious citizen gets involved in endless meetings, aimed at improving the economy, the environment, the state of the nation, or the good of his profession. At the same time, he would like to enjoy family life by staying home for a change or getting a good night's sleep. A strongly religious individual would like to follow the tenets of the church—but at the same time, values the freedom from economic pressure and from added responsibility provided by effective birth control measures.

Situations like these strap us into seemingly hopeless dilemmas and keep us from taking action. Usually, we are only dimly aware that a clash in values is our real trouble. All we know is that we feel trapped and unable to act.

What can be done about these blocks in our lives? How can we open our eyes to see and understand the habits, the values, and the fears that hobble us and prevent us from taking necessary risks to straighten out our lives? And once we see and understand, is there a cure?

Insight is the name of the game, achieving a look at yourself and your problems from a new and different perspective. Once you have learned how to step aside and see the whole picture—to reframe your situation—you will be able to act and to risk. Happily, there are many effective ways of clarifying your thinking and sorting out your emotions.

Take inventory

Writing it down, saying it out loud, are two useful and easy devices for identifying your fears, your possible conflicting values, and any other hang-ups that are stopping you from taking necessary risks.

What am I afraid of? Make a list on paper. For instance:

1. I am afraid of expressing my opinions in a group or in a meeting.
2. I am afraid of applying for a job and getting turned down.
3. I am afraid to tell my mate why our sex life is unsatisfactory. And I'm afraid to try elsewhere.

4. I'm afraid of divorce (separation) and loneliness, and yet this marriage (relationship) is making me miserable.

5. I am afraid of dogs and I cannot visit anyone who has a dog.

6. I am afraid to go on a diet, even though I am so overweight, because I'm afraid I won't be able to go through with it.

Of course, no one has all these problems. And the list is by no means exhaustive. But these are representative examples. Let us analyze these sample fears to illustrate how you can categorize your own much shorter list of problems.

Just rereading the list will make it apparent that these dilemmas are in different categories. Some are of the "I'm afraid he/she won't like me" variety. Included are numbers 1, 2, and 3. Some others are clearly involved with habits that are hard to break, like number 6. A clash of personal values may be seen in number 4. Irrational fear is illustrated by number 5.

Testing your values

Since opposing values are at the bottom of many severe personal dilemmas, it will be useful at this point to put your problems list aside and query yourself about the standards that guide your life. You already know the name of your church and the political labels with which you identify. But your daily values go far beyond those nominal associations. You probably don't (consciously) realize what those values are. And yet they pilot your existence 24 hours a day, waking or sleeping. Would you like to pin yourself down? Take pencil and paper.

1. List the highpoints of last week: people; plans made; if I could have . . .

2. Imagine a wonderful way to spend a day and then describe it.

3. List 20 things you enjoy doing.

4. Review your life: what you've accomplished, what you'd like to accomplish before you die.

5. Write your obituary: as of today, as you'd like it to read. Now write another obituary that you hope will be accurate many years hence, when your earthly course is run.

6. What have you discovered about yourself?

By looking at the results of these exercises, by pondering your own assessment of yourself, can you see how these values are related to your own inability to make progress in solving your problem(s)? For example, suppose your problem is number 4: "I'm afraid of divorce, yet this marriage is making me miserable." You value marriage as a valid institution. You value your own freedom to be yourself, without constraints. In your present situation, these values are incompatible.

Most personal dilemmas are caused by similar values clashes, whether they involve job, or marriage, or relationships with children, or obligations to parents. How does a person cope with such conflicting personal standards?

Massage the data

Massage the data! Arrange and rearrange the facts until a solution pushes itself into the foreground. You do what a counselor would do if you sat in his or her office and poured out your problems.

Let us return to the marital problem. You are the wife and you are unhappy. Ask yourself: *Why* am I unhappy? Answer: Because I feel like his slave. I'm working. He's working. But I'm doing all the work around the house. It's not a partnership, it's a prison for me. He takes me for granted. I can't talk to him about it.

Ask yourself: Why can't I talk to him about it?

Answer: He wouldn't listen anyway. I hint but I can't get through to him. And besides, we were both brought up to do it this way. It's just that I hate it.

Tell yourself: "Brought up this way?" Does this mean that you really think you ought to be doing all the housework? Is that a value you hold dear? Who taught you that?

Answer: That's how it was in my home when I was a child.

Ask yourself: So you see your husband as equivalent to your father, and you as equivalent to your mother?

Answer: Well, yes.

Question: So you're afraid to talk back to your husband, to question his way of doing things, because you're really talking back to your father?

Answer: Well, sort of.

Question: What do you imagine would be the outcome if you did challenge your husband?

Answer: Well, my father would be furious if my mother did that.

Comment: Aren't you confusing yourself with your mother and your husband with your father?

Answer: Well, I suppose . . .

Question: Would you rather stay miserable or could you take a small chance, a very little risk, and have a quiet conversation with your husband? Start with something little. Ask him: "Would you mind drying the dishes tonight? I'd like the company." Take a small risk. Do it little by little. Find out what happens. Maybe you're not married to your father after all. Maybe your husband isn't married to your mother!

The system works with any risk-taking problem. The steps are:

Report the experience or the problem.

Take your own history.

Ask yourself what you imagine to be the consequences of the step you fear to take.

Ask yourself where you got the data on which you are failing to act.

Take a small risk in the direction you'd like to go. And then take another. And another!

Dealing with fears and bad habits

Almost any kind of fear or bad habit can also be conquered with successive doses of gradualism. The basic technique is called behavior modification, a tool devised and successfully employed by behavioral psychologists. Caution: certain fears—neuroses—are so disabling that the sufferer should not fool around with self-cure. See a qualified professional. But it is entirely possible for a motivated individual to deal, without outside assistance, with some everyday fears by using the same curative principles.

Progressive desensitization is the tried-and-true method these experts employ. What you do is teach yourself little by little, taking nibbles instead of large bites out of the "forbidden" behavioral dish that you are yearning to sample but afraid to touch.

Suppose you are afraid of speaking before a group. Giving yourself a pep talk will probably not work. Rather, give a talk to one person only—a friend, an intimate, even a sympathetic acquaintance. Admit to this person that you are using him or her for practice. Say why you are doing it. And give your talk or report or statement to this safe audience of one.

This is the warm-up for an audience of, say, half a dozen. Invite your own guests. Tell them, after coffee or a drink, that this is your parlor game. And make your little speech.

Now you are almost ready for the presentation to the club or to the class or to the committee or to the office meeting. Volunteer—but do it in advance, so you will have time for preparation. And *be* prepared. Write it all out beforehand, if necessary. Put it on three-by-five cards, easily handled, carefully numbered. Or, use notes, written on the same kind of cards. When you start, mention pleasantly that this is your maiden effort at public speaking. Get the audience on your side. Joke about your props (your notes). Flatter them by taking them into your confidence. They'll smile sympathetically. And you're off to a good start.

Reexperience the problem

Thus far, we have tried to encourage ourselves in risk taking through a program of self-analysis. Reason with yourself, we have been saying. Examine your situation. Take a hard look at the pros and cons. Adopt a considered policy of gradualism in coping with fears. Massage the data. Understand your values. Talk to yourself!

But the most remarkable and most useful path toward self-understanding and risk taking has yet to be mentioned. That road is called: reexperience the problem. Instead of going forward, go back. Relax. Close your eyes. Now relive a past experience that is related to your inability to act. Stop conscious control. Image! Let it happen!

Tap your past. What happened to you way back that constricts your ability to act today? Let your past experience flash on the screen of your consciousness. Did it happen when you were a child? In school? In a family setting? What happened to you in the past that is related to what is troubling you now?

Example: A young woman had a chance to change jobs, to go into management. She feared the risk. "I'm afraid of authority. I'm actually afraid of my present boss. I wouldn't be good at it." She wanted the promotion, the increased salary, the chance for a greatly enhanced career. But—she was afraid.

The counselor she consulted told her: Relax! Image! Go back!

And the young woman took the path that was suggested. On that road she saw her older brother, a dominating fellow who had often made her childhood fearful. He made her mind, punished her when she didn't. Insight was instantaneous now. It flashed on the screen of her mind. Her brother was authority and, as a child, she couldn't fight back!

Wonderingly, relieved, the young woman reported to her counselor: "I don't need to cope with my brother any more. I'm grown up. Now I *can* fight back. I couldn't then."

She took the job. It was no longer a risk.

To expedite the imaging process, go back to the five paragraphs you wrote in Chapter 2. Therein lie the clues to what is hanging you up, the help you need to identify the crucial area.

Are you, for example, afraid of expressing opinions in a group situation? Well, then, think of the last time you confronted this problem. Go back to the experience as a participant. Have an imaginary dialogue with the people who were there. Give yourself two chairs. In one chair, speak (or fail to speak) as you did then. In the other chair, speak as your own adversary. Tell yourself off!

Is your problem rooted in conflicting values? Go back to an early experience when your values did clash. Use the same two-chair technique with that memory. Or call a pretend family meeting centering about that experience. The family consists of your various selves, or even actual members of your family. Ask the advice of those individuals. What should you do in your current dilemma? Whose advice do you find the most compelling? Does it lead you to take the risk that both tempts and repels you?

If divorce is on your mind, will you opt for continuing misery or a showdown with your mate or possible future loneliness? If you are driven by ambition to work harder than your physical or spiritual resources allow, should you keep on striving, or don't you need to prove yourself anymore? Whatever your alternatives, can you get yourself off dead center? Can you stop resisting yourself?

Consult your past. Reexperience a part of your life. Talk things over with your inner selves. And you may find a way to take a risk—if the risk finally makes sense to your inner selves.

Successful riskers

Are you still hesitating? It may give you courage to learn that many others have leaped over the chasm of their own fears, habits, and value conflicts. They did not drown. Instead they achieved better lives for themselves. Gail Sheehy has recently written an entire book portraying successful riskers.* Here are two everyday examples from our own files.

Pathfinders New York: William Morrow & Company, Inc., 1981.

Marietta, aged 52. Married at 20 to a young professor, dropped out of college herself, began having babies, keeping house, the perfect homemaker and faculty wife. The children grew up. Her husband's eminence increased. Her role of homemaker had long since become perfunctory. She was deep in her husband's shadow. In fact, she felt like a nonperson. The romance in her marriage was only a dim memory. She considered her values: a woman's place is in the home? But—not these days. Passion is not for the middle-aged. But—why not? Only the college-educated get jobs, and certainly not all of a sudden, at 52.

Marietta took multiple risks. Risking her life-style, she enrolled in one of the new undergraduate programs for mature returnees to the campus (evening classes, special curriculum, credit for the fruits of life experience). She literally dragged her husband to a marriage counselor (risking her marriage). Pending receipt of her belated bachelor's degree, she found a job running a real estate office, risking her own fears about her inability to join the "grown-up" world. Happy ending: it all worked out. Bachelor's degree, new job, reinvigorated marriage, an amazed and happy husband.

Luke, aged 33. College graduate, with honors. A veteran of the drug scene. Vegetating in a job as a security guard. Too late to rejoin the world? Unable to hold a responsible job? He told himself: "I'm too old. It's too late. I'm burned out." How could he risk doing anything substantial with his life, particularly in the light of the forbidding (to him) success of his financier father?

Luke became his own counselor. He recalled his childhood clashes with his overwhelmingly competent father. Now he dared to grow up, to risk new failure. He risked his pride and asked for his father's advice about working in the financial world. At his father's suggestion, he entered a training program for bankers. His father was not censorious, only delighted to be helpful. Luke easily survived the training program and took his place as a member of the middle class, less than a year after he decided to make the big change.

These are homely tales, but there are many others. Each of us has the ability to take risks, when needed, if we will only come to terms with inner selves who (if not heeded) still tie us down to unrewarding lives.

Is that all there is to it?

Not necessarily.

Your inner selves may have exceptionally strong minds of their own, as we shall see in the next chapter.

6

Mind-Sets

SO NOW YOU KNOW that to solve any life problem, you must be the daring young (old) man (woman) on the flying trapeze: you must take risks. But not just any old risk. If you are floundering in your present job, it will not help to risk life and limb by riding a surfboard on a windy day off the coast of Hawaii. Your risks must be related to your mind-sets. In fact, your risks will be to break out of whichever mind-set ties you down and prevents you from living a fulfilled existence.

Mind-sets?

What are mind-sets?

What is your mental picture of yourself? Self-image is a mind-set. What role do you expect your spouse to play in your marriage? Expectations are mind-sets. Do you believe that going to college is essential for success in life? Personal values are mind-sets. Does it seem to you that multinational corporations (or leftist conspiracies) are entirely responsible for the troubled state of the world? This is selective perception, also a mind-set. Prejudices are mind-sets and so are habits.

Mind-sets are our own unique way of looking at the world: at ourselves, at our various family members, at those we deal with, at life in general. By means of our mind-sets, we are able to interpret and make some kind of sense not only of our existence but also of the happenings in the community, the nation, the universe. Mind-sets weld us to our own religion, or to none at all. They make us Republicans, Democrats, communists, anarchists, pessimists, optimists, shy, outgoing, macho, embittered. In short, mind-sets are personal prescription glasses through which each of us views existence.

We all have a multitude of mind-sets. Together, they constitute our own peculiar set of maps that guide us through our daily lives. To wipe out all those mind-sets would be to render us helpless and unable to function. And yet one or more of these mind-sets may be so faulty, so unrealistic, that they are causing us to lose our way in the midst of our own lives.

Does this sound melodramatic? But it is literally true. Here are some examples.

The worm in the apple: faulty mind-sets

1. Seth's family was musical. They loved opera, symphony, making music by playing and singing together at every possible opportu-

nity. Seth studied two instruments as a child, majored in music in college with a minor in math. He was destined for a musical career, he thought. And yet the music conservatory to which he applied for further training turned down his application. The quartet in which he was playing got too few paying engagements even to cover the cost of broken strings. He failed the audition at the local symphony orchestra. Now he has a fairly good job working for a certified public accountant. But he is miserable. He is a musician—doing bookeeping!

2. Grace, at 28, is tied to the care of her mother, a widow. She has few dates because her mother needs so much attention. An older sister has gone through two marriages in a short time and is too busy with her own life to do more than visit—rarely. Grace is infuriated with her sister, rebellious at having to spend so much time with her mother (whom she really dislikes), unhappy with her paltry social life, which has mostly consisted of much older, married men. If only her father were alive! She misses his loving concern. He would have kept her from all this unhappiness.

3. Frank is an engineer employeed by a big electronics company. For some reason he cannot understand, his career is at a standstill. No promotions come his way. So he has enrolled in a graduate management program in the hope that he will learn something that will help him move along professionally. "I'm a good engineer; my talents are with machinery," he tells his professor. Frank is assigned to give an oral report on a subject of his own choosing. Reluctantly (because it is required) he gives the class a lucid 30-minute account of a complex machine with which he is working. To his surprise, he elicits spontaneous applause. "That's the first time I ever was able to understand something like that," comments a fellow student.

All three of these good people are victims of their own self-image. Seth, the failed performer, sees himself only as a musician. He has a strong mind-set that he should be making music. Therefore, any other job looks to him like failure. How can a musician do anything else but play an instrument? If Seth can break out of his mind-set he will see that he, like every other individual, has many selves. He is, in fact, quite good at math. It is not inappropriate for him to work for a CPA. Or maybe he could go into computer work. He could still be a musician in his recreational hours. He probably is not really a musician of professional caliber. Why not be an appreciator, like his family, and make his living as something else? He must change his mind-set. He must come to see himself in any one of several other vocational roles, all of them compatible with his ability and his interests.

Poor Grace! Her loving father led her into the mind-set that only older men would find her lovable. Grace's mother and sister, jealous of Grace's close attachment to her father, disliked Grace and bulwarked Grace's self-image as an unlovable woman. Now Grace is trying to buy her mother's love by lavishing time and care on the actually quite able-bodied old lady. Grace also makes herself accessible only to older married men. If only she could discard her destructive self-image, her mind-set that she is unlovable, that she alone is responsible for the care of her mother, that life is impossible without her deceased father. Then she could move out, open herself to more suitable romantic outlets, cast out her feelings of guilty responsibility, and begin to live!

Engineer Frank is not all there is to Frank. His mind-set is that he is "good" only with machinery. But actually he could be a fine communicator. When forced, he explained brilliantly—in words, which he had ruled out of his life—a complex scientific construct. To move into management, he needs to discard the false mind-set that he is a mute scientist. If he sees himself as much more, speaks up more in meetings, he will reveal his potential and very likely achieve advancement.

Small disappointments

Whole lives, like Frank's, Grace's and Seth's, are at stake as the result of destructive mind-sets. Not all of us are in so much jeopardy. But still, in almost everyone's daily experience come episodes that illustrate the casual damage resulting from tunnel vision and limited perspective; in short, from mind-sets.

You go on a trip, expecting good weather. It pours for four solid days. You had expected to play tennis, swim, and take long walks. You sulk in your hotel room and leave early, your vacation ruined. If you had been able to break out of your mind-set, you would have made an active effort to find fellow bridge players; to enjoy the old movies the hotel provided; to put on a raincoat and discover the delights of rain-hiking; to rent a car and go see the sights in spite of the weather.

You pay four dollars for a movie, expecting a Message. But the film turns out to be a light hearted spoof. You are so offended you walk out in the middle. Yet that same film got rave reviews from critics who rightly judged it as clever comedy.

You have a blind date. The girl is dark, not blond. She has a Southern accent, and you've always had a prejudice against Southern accents. The evening is a failure. Your disappointment shows and you never give her a chance to reveal her delightful sense of humor.

Mind-sets can help

None of this means that all mind-sets are harmful to health and happiness. Indeed, nobody can function without them. Mind-sets are maps, transportation, and efficiency in daily life. Our mind-sets make it unnecessary to constantly re-create our lives. Without mind-sets we would have to make decisions all day every day. Mind-sets give us a frame of reference, a means of functioning semiautomatically in repetitious situations. Mind-sets get us up in the morning at the usual time, remind us without thinking that we love our husbands or wives, turn on the ignition key in the automobile, and find our way to the office, the market, or the restaurant.

Mind-sets can also be extremely helpful in nonroutine situations. It takes a strong positive mind-set for a student to ignore all disturbances and pay attention to the essential task of studying for a final exam. A positive mind-set can improve a person's golf game, or cause him to have a good time at a party. Mind-sets are self-images, selective perception, and expectations. They are self-fulfilling prophecies. Never underestimate the power of positive thinking.

The corollary is also true. Never underestimate the power of negative thinking. Such as: I am unlovable. Or, I don't deserve to be successful. Or, this is something I'm not going to be able to do. Or, hard luck follows me wherever I go.

Where do all these mind-sets come from? And how can they be changed?

Right brain vs. left brain

Current psychological theory not only says that mind-sets can be changed but explains where they originate. According to clinical research, mind-sets that could inordinately limit one's options are probably all a product of left-brain thinking. Researchers believe that the two sides of the brain have different functions. The left brain is logical, reasonable, scientific, but also quite limited. To the left brain, a spade is a spade. But the right brain is creative, imaginative, holistic, artistic, musical, unlimited in its possibilities. Fantasy resides in the right brain.

A left-brain-dominated artist would make a representational drawing as precise as most black and white photographs, showing every wrinkle in a face, every fold in a dress. But from the right brain come the impressionists who dare to dream, to imagine, to transcend what appears on the surface.

What has this to do with you? You, like all of us, are a product of a left-brain society. We have been reared to pay the highest respect to machinery, numbers, precision, straight columns and straight thinking. In our personal lives we tend to accept the obvious, never to question the conventional wisdom and prejudices we have absorbed from our families and our schools and the environment in general. Creativity— an unconventionally furnished living room, an occupation that deviates from the family norm, a marital relationship that differs from the expected—all these are discouraged. We try to live according to socially accepted standards, we block out all but conventional notions of good and evil, right and wrong. We deny the potential of the right side of our brains.

Mind-sets are created in the left brain. And through these mind-sets our choices are automatically limited. Therefore, to get the most out of our lives, we need to give rein to our right brain, to fantasize our way out of our own rigid and self-destructive ways of looking at ourselves and the world.

This is not to say that we must consider becoming lawbreakers and social pariahs. It only means that if we unloose our imaginations we can create alternatives to our present constricted thinking and living patterns that could liberate us from our problems.

You must unfreeze your rigid mind-sets if they are getting in your way. You must seek new perspectives. And then—refreeze the new attitudes you have created so that they can be used in your newly changed life.

Easier said than done? No, not easy. But yes—it can be done.

Discovering your own mind-sets

How do you go about solving the problems of your own life?

Select an area of your life where change would be desirable. For example:

You are a woman stuck in a routine secretarial job. The company is growing. There ought to be more that you could do to move up to greater responsibility and better pay. But so much of the firm's work has to do with figures—and you're a math idiot.

You are a person who has never gotten along with your in-laws. You can't seem to communicate with them. This makes it hard on your spouse, who has always been close to the family and would like to continue to be that way. But these relatives are always discussing one another's affairs. You can't give them the chance of meddling in your business.

You are a middle-aged individual who knows you should lose at least 30 pounds for the sake of health and reasonable life expectancy. But, for you, food equals pleasure. You see yourself as a happy gourmet— fat, but nevertheless happy.

You may safely assume that a mind-set has created any of these three situations, or almost any other problem in your own life.

So what mind-set is *your* stumbling block?

Sit yourself down in a comfortable chair at home, in a room with no one else present, with no distractions from radio, television, neighbors, or family. You are alone with yourself. It is time to unleash your creative, unconventional right brain.

Unroll in front of you an imaginary video screen. Make it a wide screen, as big as one you might see in a popular bar. The figures you want to watch, and to listen to, will be nearly life-size, in color.

Now turn the switch that will reveal an episode in your life, one that you remember with emotion, with concern, one that illustrates the personal problem you have been unable to solve. Choose any scene that is relevant. Don't try to think of words to describe what you are seeing—the right brain, which is governing this adventure, is wordless, but excels in feelings and emotions.

Does the problem relate to your marriage? Flash on your screen a recent happening involving you and your spouse.

Is your difficulty job-related? Look back on an episode in your workplace that brought out all your frustrations.

Is there something wrong with your social life? Go back to any time when your difficulties were painful.

Replay conflict, loneliness, sorrow, misunderstanding, ineptitude, shame, failure—whichever memory is a distressing illustration of your troubles. If you can't see the episode at first, just hear it, or feel it, or even smell it. Accept whatever comes. It doesn't matter what channel it comes in on. And if you get stuck on a channel that has no picture, or no sound, let your right brain switch to another channel.

Go back to your childhood, or to an episode years ago, if your instinct takes you there. Relive the whole experience, see it on the screen, no matter how much it hurts you. And if the picture shifts, let it. Particularly encourage a shift to an image in the early part of your life when you experienced the same feelings.

Any images that appear on your screen are valid and relevant. Trust yourself and go with what you are visualizing or hearing. This is your experience, your life, your problem. Never mind the precise instructions you are reading here, if your inner self is impelled to do otherwise. The experiences you have chosen to relive are no accidents—they mean something.

Now imagine yourself out of the chair in which you have been attending to the screen. Be a critic, a detached observer. Watch yourself watching the screen. You are yourself, and yet not quite the same person who sits in the chair.

The detached observer asks him/herself some crucial questions:

What do you think of the person and the experience that the person in the chair has re-created? What sort of person is this sufferer? What is this agonized self doing to him/herself? What is being done to the other actors in the personal drama that has been unfolded? What weaknesses have been revealed? What strengths?

What do you see now that you missed before? What was incomplete about your recollections? What should have happened in that childhood incident that would have made you feel better, less distressed? Does that give you a clue to the meaning of your present problem?

Now dig even deeper.

What is the real problem illustrated by the scene or scenes you have just played out? The apparent problem is usually not the real problem. For instance, you may think your problem is loneliness, but perhaps you are demontrating false pride.

What alternatives did you have, what other way could you have behaved in the events you have just re-created? (Maybe you were silent, and could have spoken. Maybe you argued with the wrong person. Perhaps you should have resigned on the spot, instead of swallowing your hurt.)

Think of the episode you have screened as an unfinished movie. What would have given you a sense of completion? (Confronting your sister with your anger? Telling your mother you were going to move out?)

What assumptions did you make during the event you have just remembered so vividly? (Did you assume that your son would have to finish college regardless of his own inclinations? Did you assume that only your sister stood between you and freedom from your mother's care? Did you assume that you had no skill with words?) Are these assumptions necessarily valid?

How was the childhood picture you saw related to your present problem? (You saw yourself as a small child, being reprimanded by your mother for shutting the door to your room. Are you equating your mother with your husband's mother?)

What did the experience you recalled really say about you and the other participants? (A teacher remarked, giving you back your math test paper: "Don't be upset, all the girls have trouble with these problems." Was this teacher's bias being absorbed as gospel by you?)

Trust yourself. You *will* get a different perspective on what was happening on the screen. You *will* get a new insight. You *will* identify the mind-set that impelled the chief actor on the screen (you) to feel such great distress.

One man's story

Let us watch a man who turned on his personal video drama. This was Vern, a man in his 40s who had stumbled through two marriages and whose third marriage was now in jeopardy. On his screen he viewed a searing argument with his present wife. Only it was no argument. She raved and ranted. He was silent, aloof. Inside, the man on the screen was seething, but he said nothing while his wife poured out her wrath.

When he became a detached but interested observer, Vern had a new image: a similar silent quarrel with his second wife. A flash of insight made him realize that in all of his marriages he had been afflicted with overemotional, overexpressive wives. And in all cases he had contained his emotions, though he suffered inside.

Now another memory appeared on his screen: his father, barricaded behind a newspaper while family life flowed around him. How he had resented his father's lack of interest, his unresponsiveness! Yet he admired the man, wanted to live up to his (unspoken) standards. And he had, indeed, lived up to father's silence. He had adopted his father's mind-set: a man keeps it to himself, only a woman pours it all out.

Now the man in the chair understood that he, himself, had been throttling all his marital relationships. His wives had expressed his unexpressable emotions, thereby making themselves hateful to him. His mind-set had prevented him from participating in the emotional give-and-take of an intimate relationship. "Maybe I should let go?" the man in the chair asked himself. "It would feel so good to let her have it!"

Vern happened to be like many men in our society, good men, good husbands, good fathers, good providers, good citizens. Yet all are emotionally crippled by the sexual sterotype handed down by the Victorians and still far more prevalent than most of us will admit. A man does not show emotion. A man does not cry. A man does not mix it up verbally with his children, with his wife, with his boss, with his employees. A man functions in dignity and with judicial calm. He keeps his feelings to himself. In fact, he denies to himself that he has feelings. Emotions are unmasculine, not macho. The only time a man can let it all out is at a football game, a prize fight, a horse race, a political rally. Throw the bum out! Hit him harder! Run, you nag! Reds! Kill! Only the wife cries at a funeral. She cries for her husband, too.

The macho, show-no-emotion mind-set makes life hard for everybody, but especially for the male bogged down in "appropriate masculine behavior." The mind-set stops him from ventilating his feelings, prevents him from settling honest differences that arise with family, friends, and associates, keeps him from letting off steam except at an athletic event. It can destroy his sleep, destroy his marriage, and destroy his children. Only when he sees (on the imaginary screen) what his mind-set is doing to him can he think about discarding or changing his mind-set and saving his life.

How it works for others

Here is how the video screen technique could work for the secretary whose mathematical inability prevents her from getting a better job. She sees herself at work. She reviews her co-workers and her immediate supervisor. She notes with her usual envy the rather stupid woman who is in charge of inventory and who rates her own private office.

Now she moves to the side and watches herself watching the screen. She feels anger. "Why can't I do *her* job? Because I'm no good at arithmetic?" She has a new image of the teacher unsmilingly handing back her test paper. "I'm not good at arithmetic? Just because he said so? I gave up long ago, didn't I? Is it too late? Maybe I could get a calculator, one of those pocket-size ones. . . ."

She can, indeed, learn a math-related job. Her mind-set, unfortunately, was math anxiety, peculiar to many women in our society. They think they can't do math; it's their mind-set. So of course they can't.

Consider the man with the weight problem. He views himself on the video screen eating a wonderful dinner. Fresh bread and sweet butter. Steak with bearnaise sauce. Green salad with a delicious oil dressing. Strawberry shortcake. What bliss!

He calls up his childhood and sees his mother, beaming at him as he ate every morsel on his plate. What a wonderful cook she was! He smells the bread baking in the long-ago kitchen. Food, he realizes, represented love, security, approval. Does he still need that kind of security?

Letting his imagination run free, he now has a mental image of an admired friend playing tennis and winning. A slim friend. Shall he think like a fat man and take seconds? Or think like a thin man and smilingly pass up the rolls and the butter and the dessert, concentrating on a showy tennis game instead? Which self—which mind-set—will win the internal contest? It's a matter of values, he realizes. Does he value food and the false feeling of security more than life and ultimate well-being?

The person who has trouble talking to his in-laws also takes himself to a meal, a Thanksgiving dinner in his wife's family's home. What a good time everybody is having, talking, laughing. He sees himself as a silent outsider, a lonely-looking figure. He sees that he was left out of the jolly give-and-take. It wasn't much fun for him, that Thanksgiving. Obviously, it was his own doing.

He recalls Thanksgiving in his own childhood home, a far different, warmer occasion. How much his family means to him! He has always felt guilty about living so far away from them, changing allegiance, becoming part of a different circle of relatives. Insight comes. He has a sense of disloyalty whenever he is with his in-laws. And now he sees that he has assumed all along that his wife's relatives were trying to woo him away from his own kin. Now it seems like a rather foolish notion. Would it hurt to give this other family a chance? He has a momentary vision of himself exchanging joking, friendly insults with his brother-in-law. Why not?

One more example:

You are a person who is almost always lonely, even in a crowd. Parties are an agony for you. You never have anything to say to anyone. You take a drink or two to loosen up but it gives you a headache almost immediately. Besides, you can never remember later what you said under the influence of alcohol and you worry about having made a fool of yourself. Now you view yourself at one of these parties.

What is your mind-set? Your mind-set is that it is dangerous to reveal yourself to anybody because you are uninteresting, sometimes foolish, and nobody would care anyway.

Be honest. (Nobody is listening to your inner voice but you.) You have another mind-set as well. You believe you are really smarter than everybody else. But if you revealed that clever self at a party then for certain nobody would be willing to talk to you. They'd feel outclassed and envious.

Who else should be at that party? You are visualizing your brother. See how he socializes with one and all, chatting, laughing, always with the right answers and the right anecdotes. A good dancer, too. Good-looking. Well-dressed. What was it your mother said, when you both were little? "Joe has so many friends, he's a natural." You were reading a book at the time. She looked at you and she sneered a little. You remember it so well. Could it have been a sneer? She did love you, didn't she? It looked like a sneer. And she did say that about Joe. Did it have anything to do with you? Well, let's admit it. She wasn't criticizing you. But, at the time, you thought she was. It happened a lot, didn't it? Did it? Here is another mind-set. Mother preferred Joe, loved him more. Did she really? Well, you thought so, when you were a child.

What good is it to act the way you do now? Easy: it conceals—everything! Wouldn't it be better to take a chance at being a bit foolish? You're afraid people won't respect your brains if you say something ordinary. But maybe they won't notice one way or another. After all, people are really just interested in themselves. Could you start by asking them questions about themselves? Could you risk telling them about yourself in the course of the conversation? What could you really lose? Are you actually so uninteresting? Are you sure everyone prefers Joe? Are you genuinely smarter than anyone else? Are people apt to feel envious of you even if you are brighter than they are? Admit it—we're all bright, in different ways. Nobody's going to be envious. It's just your mind-set that they are. Will the heavens fall if you speak to a stranger at a party? NO!

A guided tour

In order to solve any personal problem by using your own inner resources, it is essential for you to take a guided tour of your own mind-sets. You need not catalog all your mind-sets, only those that are causing difficulty in your life. Therefore, you must zero in on the particular mind-sets that are giving you trouble.

Using the video screen technique (or any introspective posture that suits you better), get a clear mental picture of yourself and of your particular predicament. Ask yourself searching questions, including these:

What do you think is your mind-set in the area that is troubling you?

Do you, perhaps, have more than one mind-set in that area?

Are you looking at only one part of the picture?

Are there other figures that should be present and that play a part in your problem? Your mother? Your father? A sister or brother? A teacher?

Think back to an event in your childhood and flash it on your video screen. Choose an event that might be related to your current difficulties.

What are you gaining by your present behavior? What are the disadvantages?

Are there other ways to achieve those values?

Give your right brain permission to fantasize. Imagine behavior opposite to the way you have been acting recently.

Imagine how someone else might behave in the same situation. What would happen if *you* behaved that way? Imagine the implications.

Is there a middle road? You can find out in the next chapter.

7

*Balancing
Your
Act*

ARE YOU THE WAY you think you are?

Are you really the perfect old-fashioned wife and mother, someone who is the pillar of the family and nothing more?

Are you really the glad-handing salesman everybody knows, comfortable with one and all, the total extrovert?

Are you really a consummately rational and realistic scientist, not one for emotionality and airy-fairy notions?

Strange as it may seem, the way you think you are—scholar, saint, salesman, philosopher—is not all of you. Indeed, within your unconscious is the *opposite* of the individual you believe you are.

You may see yourself as a rational scientist. But buried within, surfacing only in your dreams, is a feeling, emotional self who would like to be walking on a beach on a South Sea island.

Your conscious identity may be an unliberated housewife, mother, and grandmother. But if you could interview your unconscious, you might find a potential corporation president with a secretary to bring *you* coffee on demand.

You may see your role in the world as a straitlaced moralist and prim churchgoer. But how about your dreams: do you make love to your neighbor's spouse or frequent a garish disco as you sleep?

Every conscious attitude has its opposite in the unconscious. Philosophers and psychologists believe this to be a fact of life. Hegel, the philosopher, taught that for every thesis there is an antithesis. Giving due weight to each, he said, leads to synthesis, or balance.

Similarly, when our lives are unhappy, we must suspect that we are not synthesizing the opposite tendencies that dwell within us. One aspect of our selves is dominant, the opposite suppressed. We are unbalanced.

Imbalance is everywhere

The world is full of unbalanced people—unbalanced, unhappy people. No, they are not insane, nor even slightly weak in the head. Yet they suffer severely from a lack of equilibrium in the way they lead their lives. They persist in behaving in a way that is not in their own self-interest. Single-purpose people are prime illustrations of imbalance and unhappiness.

A writer lives like a nun or a monk, cloistered with thoughts and feelings, working alone, producing good work, but achingly lonesome.

A wife gives and gives in a one-sided relationship with her husband, serving, placating, deferring to his wishes. She never asks, and she seldom receives.

An engineer views himself and all the world like a gigantic computer. He is always trying to force all relationships and all problems into mathematical formulas. The severely rational approach doesn't always work in his life but he keeps on stubbornly trying.

A convinced religious fundamentalist interprets everything that happens from the rigid perspective of an ideology. Like Marxists, political rightists, and other ideologues, the fundamentalist suffers constant frustration because the world persists in deviating from the "rules."

These are only a few examples of how people live unbalanced, unsatisfactory lives, captives of their own restricted mind-sets. Personal relationships, work, learning, one's place in the community—one or the other becomes skewed and unsatisfying when a person deals with life in an unbalanced fashion. In extreme cases, the individual whose existence is out of equilibrium wakes each morning with a feeling of dread. Something is always missing. Something is always wrong.

It may appear that "unbalanced" people are merely answering the dictates of their own essential nature. True—but a self has more than one natural inclination. By suppressing all but one dominant characteristic, these people are making themselves wretched.

Lack of balance is a major cause of personal unhappiness. Most of us are somewhat unbalanced in the way we deal with our lives. And most of us are unaware of just what is bothering us. A simple rule of thumb can give you a clue to imbalance. Your life is lopsided when "the way you are" doesn't make you happy.

Elsa, the giver

Consider Elsa, an introspective sort of woman whose unhappiness in her marriage has driven her to seek counseling. This is not her first failed marriage. She has had no less than two others. "Why," she asks the counselor, "am I attracted to men who are takers? All my husbands, especially this one, expect me to provide everything: service in all household matters, unselfish submission in bed, sacrifice of my own interests to theirs in every aspect of daily life. I run his errands, I keep dinner warm until he chooses to show up. I even buy his clothes. All this, while I hold down an outside job too! Do I even get a compliment from him when I wear something new? No! I'm his slave, without even a thank-you."

Talking it over with the therapist uncovers a telling history. Elsa was the only girl in a family of boys, a bookish child who was always left out of everything. Her exclusion from the lively activity of the family had caused her to seek refuge in reading and to think of herself as an unattractive, socially inept sort of person. It also taught her that the way to get her brothers' attention and approval was to buy them off—to give out payola. She performed services for them, did their chores, shined their shoes, and even shared her allowance with them. When she grew up, her image of herself persisted. So did her loneliness. And so did her ready solution: payola to the men she married to restore her sense of self-worth.

Elsa's demeaning marriages were, of course, her own doing. As long as she persisted in such relationships, she was fated to suffer anger and unhappiness. She had failed to honor that inner self who needed to be a receiver, a potentially social self with something to offer besides payola.

Such lack of balance in relationships is as unhealthy as lack of balance in one's diet. To be the constant giver, never a taker (or vice versa) is as damaging as a diet of all meat and never any fruit or vegetables. Just as one must keep the wheels of an automobile in balance, so must one keep watch on equilibrium in relationships.

The workaholic

Imbalance in work is no less unhealthy. Workaholics illustrate perfectly a hard truth—imbalance may be socially useful but personally destructive. Consider Vincent, who owned a retail store with fixed hours but who nevertheless usually found it necessary to stay late, go to work early, pick up loose ends all day Sunday. He missed meals, was late to family occasions, left the children's rearing almost entirely to his wife.

Vincent was taught early to feel guilty when he was not working. As a teenager, he had been employed part-time by his father. He told a revealing anecdote about that period in his life. One Saturday he was at the family store as usual but there was really nothing to do.

"Why aren't you working?" demanded his father. When the boy shrugged, the father picked up a box of thumbtacks and dumped them on the floor. "Now you have something to do!"

Thus was guilt about idleness built into Vincent. He could not rest unless he was working, even though the work might be unessential or not at all urgent. He made his life lopsided in order to assuage his anxious conviction that work was the supreme good, even if it was work for the sake of work.

Vincent had suppressed the self that would have enjoyed leisure, recreation, just plain loafing. He denied those impulses entirely. While depriving not only himself but also his neglected family, he truly believed that "I'm only happy when I'm working." When he dragged himself off to work, dead tired, he thought his problem was too little sleep. But it was really depression caused by living a lopsided life.

"I'm just an idiot about such things"

Imbalance also invades our schools and colleges, creating adults who are forever inadequate in vital areas. A grading system that puts a premium on A's turns out "students" who, seeking security, choose courses that will produce, if at all possible, A's

For example, the person with a natural bent for languages stays away, as much as the requirements will permit, from science, where poorer grades might spoil a good record. The student who easily does well in math steers clear of English courses. As a result, forever after the linguist "can't possibly" mend a frayed lamp cord or put together a child's disassembled toy—"I'm just an idiot about such things." Something approaching rigor mortis sets in when the mathematician has to write a business letter. And the compulsive A student is apt to grow up to be the no less compulsive expert in his or her chosen field, because only thus can the individual feel secure.

Stuffed into the unconscious, never honored by these people, are the abilities and inclinations that could make them adequate performers in the areas in which they call themselves idiots. The joys of going to a concert elude a self-created engineering type; the pleasures of building shelves for the garage escape the accountant; the scholar who allows himself to be nothing else never gets to sit down in happy camaraderie at the neighborhood bar. All these people suffer from lack of balance in their lives. What they are doing is not really in their own best interest.

Dealing with stress

Without realizing it, most of us are unbalanced in more subtle but no less damaging ways: in how we customarily deal with the stressful situations that inevitably arise in everyone's life.

Are you like Susan's mother? This was a lady whose invariable reaction to any crisis was to blame somebody else. Even when the mother herself spilled the milk when pouring it into a glass, she blamed the nearest child for upsetting her, or for shouting at an inopportune moment, or for being where he shouldn't have been. Whatever happened in that household was (according to mother) somebody else's fault.

All during her long life, this woman was a blamer, making everyone, including herself, unhappy with her complaints. Unfortunately, Susan, who abhorred her mother's blaming temperament, turned out to be a blamer also. Not so, however, Susan's brother, Al. That young man habitually reacted to crises in an exactly opposite way. He was the placater, the one who accepted his mother's blame (whether he deserved it or not) and always followed up by doing all he could to "put her in a good mood" again. As an adult, he treated coworkers, supervisors, his wife, and his children in the same "You're right—what can I do to make you feel better?" manner.

Mother, Susan, Al, all three were unbalanced in their life postures. None of the three was happy, though they couldn't understand why. To feel constantly angry—whether it is expressed by the blamer, or suppressed by the placater—is not unpleasant but counterproductive. Neither stance solves problems. Both stances make the individual unhappy. Both are essentially unbalanced ways of facing up to life.

According to psychologist Virginia Satir, not everybody is either a blamer or placater. Another pair of extreme, and thus unbalanced, ways of approaching life, are the superrational person and the individual Satir calls "distracting." A perfect illustration is provided by a certain married couple.

The superrational in this pair was a highly respected medical specialist whose work involved dissecting cadavers to discover the secrets of the illnesses or accidents that had killed them. He was the man behind the newspaper report that "an autopsy was performed and. . . ." This physician had found the right professional niche, for he was utterly without emotion as he went about his grisly work. With scientific detachment he cut into what was human flesh and organs and viewed all of it as just so much physical matter, devoid of any connection to him or to anybody else. This rational approach caused him to be not only efficient but also insulated from unpleasant feelings as he analyzed other people's mortal crises. Unfortunately, this superrational attitude carried over into the man's daily life. His feelings were so much suppressed that he could not even muster an emotional reaction to a menu in a restaurant.

"What are you having?" he asked a companion. "I'll have the same."

To whom was this clear-eyed medical man married? His absolute opposite. The doctor's spouse was a ballet dancer who had not made it. She was also a dramatic actress who had been unable to get a part in a play, a failed poet, an incompetent femme fatale. Her emotional, distracting attitudes, her posing and posturing, her intermittent gaiety and frequent sulks, were interesting at a party, but unserviceable in the extreme in either a job or a household. The doctor was attracted to all that he was not; the unemployed dancer likewise. They married but their life together was a hell and they soon divorced. He found her beguiling but impossible. She found him solid but dull and demanding. Neither was happy, either apart or together. They were suffering from temperamental imbalance.

Do you recognize yourself in any of these people? Are you always blaming—or always placating? Are you superrational, an engineer in life as well as at the office? Or are you a distracted soul, all over the lot, never focussed, always ephemeral?

We all share these characteristics, but if you carry any one of these stances too far you are out of balance and need to look deep inside yourself for a different way of responding to life's crises.

Make a survey

How do you know in what way you are out of balance? Or even if you are out of balance? Perhaps you already know: you may have recognized yourself in one or more of the examples already given. There could, however, be other means of identification. You could sit down and ponder your life, make a mental survey, keeping balance-imbalance in mind.

Some clues are obvious. For instance:

1. Have you worked hard all your life, made a good living, or run an excellent household? *But*: are you still continuing to do the same things, as diligently and as single-mindedly as ever, even though circumstances have changed: children grown up, plenty of others to help at the office, enough money to take a trip or retire, cold climate too hard on aging bones? *Why are you still working so hard*?

2. Were you an aggressive, effective soldier in Vietnam? The war's long since over. Are you still picking fights? *Why don't you put away that gun*?

3. Were you a happy scholar in college? Did you love campus life,

reading, the relaxed hours, the easy companionship? Years later, are you still ducking adult responsibilities and taking refuge in fraternity-like life at the club, or hours of reading in a library, avoiding responsibilities? *Why don't you grow up*?

4. In your late thirties, or early forties, or even mid-fifties, are you still slogging away at the same kind of work but somehow feeling unhappy and restless? Stop blaming yourself. Maybe you do need a change of career, or geography, or even new friends or a new love. *Are you married to the status quo*?

Test yourself

You can test yourself in a somewhat more structured manner to find out how and if you are living life in an unbalanced way.

One way of getting a perspective on your life is to make a systematic record of how you spend your time. Write down how you spent last Friday. Do it like a brief diary. Then write down how you spent last Saturday. Now write down how—if you had your druthers—you would like to spend Friday. Compose an imaginary Friday diary. Do the same for a future Saturday.

Now analyze the two accounts. What is different? Climate? Activities? Not working? Being with somebody different? Being alone? Doing a different job? The gap between the real and the ideal could reveal your balance problem and suggest how you might work out a compromise between the two to get more equilibrium in your life in the future.

Where are you hurting?

Another way of interviewing your balance problem is to ask yourself: Where am I hurting? A "facilitator" at a Veterans' Hospital asked that question of a group of outpatients who came for help with their unsatisfying lives. The frank public answers were revealing, not necessarily to the other people in the room but to the people who were making the honest statements.

One man's hurts were related to drugs, another's to alcohol.

Another man was hurting because of an unsatisfactory relationship with his stepfather.

A woman said: "I'm so bitchy—it makes me feel bad."

"My weight hurts me," blurted out another individual.

"Every day I have a new disease. It hurts to be a hypochondriac," one person confessed. And another reported that his hurts were bound up with his grown children, who were always taking from him, with very little evidence of gratitude.

Most of the people who write to "Dear Abby" are writing about their hurts.

None of these people have balanced lives or balanced relationships. All are unhappy. Where are *you* hurting?

Why don't you. . . ?

Dr. Victor Frankl, a psychologist, has a different device for helping an unhappy individual discover what is really eating him—and what are the pluses in life. He asks some clients, rather brutally, "Why don't you commit suicide?"

Ask yourself the same question. It will reveal the parts of you that you have been ignoring, that are worth saving, that have been left out of consideration in your unbalanced life.

Here are some more leading questions, to help you discover what's out of whack in your own life:

What part of your life isn't working for you?
What changes would you like to make?
What makes you unhappy?
Would you like to change your physical self? How?
Would you like to change your emotional self? How?

Analyzing the data

Armed with these facts, many of them matters you have never addressed before, you are now in a position to make constructive changes in your outlook on life and perhaps in the way you live your life.

First, accept the truth: that within you are infinite possibilities. Many of those possibilities you have suppressed during the course of your life, due to your upbringing and other environmental influences. But now, motivated by conscious unhappiness, you are free to delve within yourself and make use of heretofore half-conscious abilities, aspirations, and emotions.

For example: Fear and bravery reside within every one of us. Recognizing both, you can allow yourself to decide how to act under specific circumstances. You don't always need to be a hero; you don't always need to be a coward. Within a blamer, there is a placater. Whichever one you have been, you can, if you wish, now allow yourself to utilize your opposite buried tendency, when appropriate.

Inspired by the data you have unearthed about yourself, you now have some notion of how your life is pulling you out of shape. You now know the ways in which you are paying too much attention to a single aspect of your life. You now know what is preoccupying you, to the exclusion of other matters that are important to you. You now know the nature of the unfinished business in your life.

You are now also in a position to change your tactics in dealing with your problem. If you have been superrational you could make a conscious decision to dip into your emotional instincts and let some part of your fantasy life do the steering. By identifying your heretofore dominant tendency, you are free to make judicious use of the hidden opposite. In that way, you will be released from your customary responses to stress and will be able to achieve a different result.

Here is how all this could work with our hypothetical (but actually quite real) examples.

The engineer, till now rational in all things, needs to get in touch with his feelings and let them show. Boss, wife, husband, children, will respond accordingly and differently too. It's a whole new ball game.

Susan and her mother, habitual blamers, could draw on the placater within. They could tap the deep wells of sympathy or (to change the metaphor) see the view from a different mountain.

As for the wife who is a giver and has been a confirmed placater all her life, she could rebalance by trying blaming, trying rationality, bringing these and other possibilities to bear on her unsatisfactory home life.

The workaholic could allow himself to play, for a change. Or even, perhaps, to sell the store.

No one can—or should—change personalities or life-styles overnight. No one needs to go to extremes. Change must be gradual and experimental. Nor is the process of synthesizing one's opposing tendencies possible with a snap of the fingers. There are ways of trying out, little by little, all the hidden potential that till now has been deep in your unconscious. Having made the decision to rebalance, having recognized the enormous possibilities in your life, you are now in a position to work on generating useful alternatives, as you will see in the next chapter.

8

Generating Alternatives: You Do Have A Choice

THIS HAPPENED 40 years ago.

Joey, aged four, was eating his lunch. Or, rather, he was not eating his lunch.

"Eat your carrots!" commanded his conscientious mother.

"I don't like carrots," Joey complained.

"If you don't eat your carrots, I'm going to send you outside without your dessert."

"Don't like carrots!" Joey insisted.

Exasperated, the boy's mother seized him roughly by the arm, opened the back door, shoved her son outside, and locked the door behind him. Whereupon the infuriated child drove his fist through a glass panel in the door.

The physical injury turned out to be minor. The mother is now dead. But the emotional effect of the incident remained with Joe into his own middle age. He still remembers the terror he felt as a four-year old, not because of the possibility of cutting his hand but in fear of the power of his own anger.

Seeing a counselor four decades later, Joe recalled the incident with a thrill of horror. But only now did he realize how profound an effect that moment of unbridled fury had had on his life. He had routinely, although unconsciously, made a practice of throttling his dangerous emotions. As a result, he had made himself, at least superficially, into a cold superrationalist who was seriously out of sync with all the important people in his life. His marriage was rocky. He was at odds with his children. And his relationships with his professional associates were poor. He had resorted to counseling because he felt he had no alternatives. He knew he needed to make changes to keep his life from sliding into an abyss. But *what* changes? He had no idea that his problems were of his own making. Nor did he have any notion what his alternatives could be.

Many roads are open

Perhaps you, too, need to make a change in your life. Perhaps, like Joe, you also are wondering if change is either possible or practical. The good news is that one need not necessarily return to the starting point—like Joe's confrontation with his childhood emotions—to make a fresh start. Having recognized that your life is hurrying along the wrong road, it is enough to accept that there must be other routes to take, smaller course corrections to be made.

Usually it is not essential to go back to the beginning and relive the searing experiences that may have pushed you to take an unfortunate turn on life's journey. See a psychologist or counselor if you will, delve deep into your past if you wish. But the chances are that you can make necessary changes all by yourself. All that is needed is to see your current problem clearly (regardless of its origin) and to understand that you have real choices in how you go about solving it.

Many despairing people think they are locked into their problems. A man hates his boss but needs to stay in the job in order to advance in his profession. A middle-aged woman puts up with her unsatisfactory marriage because the only alternative she sees is the loneliness of being all by herself. An overweight person keeps raiding the refrigerator, seemingly helpless to stop disfiguring himself and endangering his health and longevity.

Like these people, many of us feel locked in. We fail to realize that there are keys to the cage and that we already have them within our possession.

Eyes that see not

Take Joe, the superrationalist. He had been blaming his wife, his children, and his co-workers for the unpleasantness, the downright misery of his dealings with them. But he found that he had been looking at his problems without really seeing them. The counselor guided him to realize that he was defeating himself by throttling his own natural and healthy emotionality.

Take the man who dared not leave his job, even though he was at serious odds with his boss. He failed to see the real problem, that his temperament and his boss's were hopelessly incompatible. Advancement in such circumstances would never happen. Instead, he was likely one day to find his desk in the hall and be forced to leave anyway. The solution was not to hang on but to look for another position now, while still on the payroll.

As we saw in an earlier chapter, these and most other problems were actually not realistically understood by the sufferer. And if you don't see what your problem is, how can you solve it? Do you feel like a caged animal? Have you been pacing fruitlessly around the closed perimeters of your difficulty? All you need is to close your eyes, stop seeing those bars, and wake up to a new look. You say there's no window or door in the cage? You are wrong. There is both a window and a door. All you need is to learn how to find them.

A new technique

You must learn how to draw your hand, without looking at either the paper or the pencil.

Absurd? Not at all. This is a technique used by an innovative art teacher named Betty Edwards to enhance creativity and artistic confidence. But the method is precisely on target for helping individuals learn how to see what they have previously taken for granted and to use the creativity that is within all of us. The ability to see what we have previously ignored, to hear what we have previously failed to hear, is the key to creative development of ways of reassembling our lives.

Back to Betty Edwards. She has had enormous success with grown-up students who had been drawing like eight-year-olds and who only a couple of months later were producing excellent pencil portraits worthy of display in an art show. These students were by no means exceptionally talented individuals. All they had was motivation and a teacher who knew how to guide them to unlock their own heretofore buried creativity.

How does this relate to you? To draw a face or a hand, one must really see it. To solve life's problems, one must really see and feel them in all their aspects. And how can one learn to see, to hear, and to feel? It is all a matter of left brain—right brain.

As we pointed out in an earlier chapter, scientists have shown that our brains are separated into two halves, each with distinctly different functions. The left brain, which dominates in most of us, is in charge of reasoning, rationality, language ability, and the orderly processing of information. The right brain, in contrast, is the feeling side, the hemisphere that sees the whole picture rather than its component parts. The right brain is in charge of leaps of insight. It is intuitive, subjective, holistic, spontaneous. It knows no time constraints.

Experiments have shown that each side of the brain processes the same information quite differently. The left brain names an object correctly but cannot really see it, at least not well enough to make a good drawing. In contrast, the right brain, if unhindered by the preoccupations of the left brain, can draw the object very well.

This kind of special vision carries over from art work, like drawing, to the everyday problems of human relationships. What you need to do is to temporarily "unhook" your dominant left brain, with its ready-made labels and its preconceptions, and switch on your right brain with its ability to see a situation whole, unhindered by foregone conclusions and rationalizations. Then you can feed the newly realized data into your more rationalistic left brain and come up with some new answers.

Is your left brain still skeptical? Try the drawing exercise in order to understand the intense practicality of this mental dichotomy.

Do the drawing

First make a drawing of your hand without looking at it. It's easy—you've seen your hand thousands of times. You already know what your hand looks like. Now put that drawing aside. Then tape a piece of paper on the table or desk, comfortable for the hand that will draw—your right or your left, depending on which hand you normally use for writing. Now, leaving your drawing hand in position to draw, turn your body around so you are looking only at your opposite hand, of which you are assigned to make a drawing. Resist the impulse to look at the drawing; it will defeat the purpose of this exercise. Now, to quote Betty Edwards:

> *Very slowly, creeping a millimeter at a time, move your eyes along the edge of your hand, observing every minute variation and undulation of the edge. As your eyes move, also move your pencil point at the same slow pace on the paper, recording each slight change or variation in the edge that you observe with your eyes. . . . Draw the edges you see one bit at a time. . . . You will find yourself becoming fascinated with the wondrous complexity of the thing you are seeing, and you will feel that you could go deeper and deeper into the complexity. . . . Your drawing will be a beautiful record of your deep perception. We are not concerned about whether the drawing looks like a hand. We want a record of your perceptions.*

Are you surprised by the picture you have drawn? This drawing is a product of your creative right brain. Compare it to the first drawing, done under the guidance of your left brain. How much richer is the right-brain drawing! How different! You have seen characteristics of your hand of which you were never previously conscious. Wouldn't it be wonderful to see and feel new aspects of your life, until now brushed aside by your school-disciplined left brain?

If you are interested in learning to draw, you can follow up this fascinating process by buying Betty Edwards' book: *Drawing on the Right Side of the Brain* (Houghton Mifflin 1979), from which we have borrowed, with permission from the author and the publisher. For now, however, we are after not hands but hearts.

Suspend judgment and daydream

If you have faithfully done the hand-drawing exercise, you must realize that the new look at your hand was possible because you allowed yourself to suspend judgment about what a hand looks like. Similarly, you are now going to suspend judgment about your problem and about its solution. You are going to switch off the same old recorder, with the same old rationales and the same old perceptions, that has imprisoned you in the same old feelings of helplessness. Instead, you are going to turn on your feelings and daydream yourself into new insights.

Settle down in a comfortable chair. Or in the bathtub. Or on a rock at the edge of a lake. Or in bed, alone with your thoughts. Or sitting in sunlight with a hat over your eyes. Or listening to music in your own room. Or even slumped at a desk with a dull book in front of you. Do something—anything—that you associate with relaxation.

Now let your mind drift. Daydream. Be receptive to feelings, to memories, to whatever images float in front of your mind's eye. Permit emotions to surge up, whether they are resentment, or anger, or love, or regret. Wander in your mental garden. Are you seeing snails? Flowers? Dead branches? An unkempt lawn? Rows of healthy vegetables? See and feel it all. Irrelevant as some of it may seem, this is your creative right brain, telling you at long last "how it is." Trust your daydream. This is You speaking, the You you have long suppressed.

Like the drawing of your own hand, done without looking at the drawing, while daydreaming you will be drawing a new perception of the landscape of your life. Your unfettered imaginings may seem like an irrational hodgepodge of thoughts, feelings, memories, and intuitions. But within this mixture are valuable clues and directional signals. What you are doing, in effect, is brainstorming, a well-recognized technique, usually done in a group (but you are your own group now), that leads to innovative solutions to problems.

How to brainstorm

How do you brainstorm? Children and adolescents do it all the time. Think back to your early childhood, the times when you played Cinderella or cowboy or teacher or mommy and daddy. Recollect some of your adolescent fantasies, too. Maybe you wrote poetry. Perhaps you pitched sandlot baseball and pretended you were a major leaguer. This is only to remind you that you can—because you have done so in the past—entertain "crazy" ideas.

Now, in your daydreaming state, entertain some crazy ideas about your current problems. Listen to these ideas in an unprejudiced way. Accept what you are thinking even if your rational self really disagrees. In other words, turn on your creative right brain, ignoring the judgmental left brain that is tied to preconceptions and foregone conclusions.

Give yourself all the time you need to generate these crazy ideas. Just as you drew your hand without looking judgmentally at what you were drawing, so should you draw the fantasies related to your current life problems. Focus on the "I" part of your problem, not on what someone else is doing. For instance, if your problem seems to relate to your boss, leave him or her out of your thoughts now. Concentrate on yourself, how you feel, what you might like to do, what's best for you. Use guided imagery: form mental pictures of your ideas and impulses.

Here is a homely small example of a woman who consented to brainstorm a nagging problem. She is a financial consultant, busy, well respected, but chronically overworked. The immediate problem is a widowed client who comes to the consultant's office and stays and stays, complaining, asking absurd questions, taking up valuable time. One visit from this woman is so long, so aggravating, that it is enough to poison a whole working day. Unfortunately, the financial adviser has other similar clients, because of a well-deserved reputation for sympathy and patience. But this client is the worst.

The harried counselor (quite skeptical) agreed to daydream, to relive the last incident with the troublesome client, to suspend judgment, and to brainstorm. Here are the ideas that were generated.

Tell the client to go to hell.
Get up and say: "Sorry, I'm feeling sick. I can't talk to you any more."
Say: "Take your business someplace else!"
Sock her in the nose.
Say: "I've got someone in the waiting room."
Tell the client she is perfectly capable of answering all those questions herself.
Recommend a singles group.

Laugh, take her arm, and escort her firmly from the room, murmuring, "I guess I've run out of time."

At least one of those ideas—or a combination of two or more—would work. The brainstormer realizes that she has put up not only with this one pest but with a whole galaxy of pests, out of a preconceived notion that one must be infinitely polite to every individual with whom one does business. She realizes that *there are other ways* of handling these situations, short of inflicting mayhem on the clients or committing professional suicide. No longer does the businesswoman need to suffer and to waste valuable time.

Brainstorming is merely a matter of interviewing yourself, discovering what is going on in your mind. It allows you to express the heretofore unmentionable. It makes it possible to pretend that you are someone else who takes bold actions that you yourself "have never dreamed" of taking (or have you?). It allows you to take your own side of the argument for a change. It reveals alternatives and uncovers not new but heretofore concealed ideas. It shows you that almost everything in life is negotiable.

Positives and negatives

Having daydreamed and brainstormed, you are now in a position to make some lists, in the light of your new perceptions. Make two lists. Write down the positive aspects of your present situation. Also write down the negatives. For example, take this problem: "What do I do about my unhappy job?"

Positives
A good paycheck
Security
Possibility of advancement
Status
Low risk of being fired

Driving forces
Lack of self-expression—can't be myself
Too many demands on me
Incompatible interests

Incompatible temperaments
Incompatible life-style

Restraining forces
Children
Family reaction
Fear of loneliness
Maybe it'll get better
Something may be wrong with *me*?

Check out all the items for false assumptions. For example, will family really react badly? Will loneliness really ensue? Is it realistic to expect improvement? Are temperaments really incompatible (they didn't use to be)? Are all those demands unreasonable? Who am I—what do I think I have to express?

In making a survey of the elements of your problem, be sure to discard those that are out of your control. For example, you could do nothing to eliminate children from the list of your considerations (unless they are already grown). But if boredom is a problem, you can do something about that, maybe by spicing up your sex life, or by agreeing with your mate on a new joint recreational activity, like racquetball or a little-theater subscription, or joining a hiking club.

Pick out what is truly significant. For instance, incompatible life-style is not necessarily fatal to a relationship. Most people have somewhat different interests. That could make the relationship more exciting—if you let it. Or: are you sure your mate is keeping you from being yourself? Maybe you yourself are doing the suppressing. In short, don't deal with all the issues you've listed; just concentrate on the right ones. Shake loose the unconscious assumptions. Discard the unimportant. Forget the elements that really can't be changed. Do it all in the light of your new brainstormed perceptions. You will see that *everything* is possible. All you have to do is to decide which course is best for you.

The process might be called "regeneralization," as we shall see in Chapter 9, our grand finale and our new beginning.

9

How About Tomorrow?

BY NOW, YOU HAVE WORKED through eight chapters of conscientious self-analysis. You have pinpointed your problems. You have learned to trust yourself and owned up to your talents, your tendencies, your strengths, weaknesses, needs, and aspirations. You have accepted the need to take risks in order to realize your goals. At this juncture, you are aware of the destructive power of certain mind-sets. As a grand finale, you now clearly understand the alternatives among which you can pick and choose in order to live a balanced, satisfying and self-fulfilled life.

Does this mean that all your troubles are over, that from this time forward you've got it all together, forever and ever (amen)?

Not quite. Life is not nearly so neat. No one stays "happy" or well balanced indefinitely. Were it so, we would quickly expire of boredom, or at least boredom would become the problem. Change is the constant in every existence.

For one thing, our outward circumstances change. For another, change comes from within, as we age, as our needs change, as our associations change, as we broaden (or narrow) in our aspirations, our interests, our capacities. Nothing is static. In short, if you think you are now done with challenge and difficulty, disabuse yourself. You are not. And, God willing, you never will be—not, at least, until death does you part from earthly concerns.

Ages and stages

Psychologists and philosophers have confirmed what we all already know, if you stop to think about it. Any life goes through stages, depending on chronological development and current circumstances. An entire academic discipline has been constructed concerning the changes in children's development. As youngsters mature, they change continually. Their capacities grow; their psychological condition changes. Growing up is the name of the game. As every parent knows, there's never a dull moment, never a time when it is possible to relax in face of the daunting job of bringing up a baby. Our great-grandmothers wisely sighed: "Little children, little problems; big children, big problems."

And so it is with ourselves. Our problems vary as we grow older, although less predictably than the well-worked-out stages of children and adolescents. Still, adult developmental stages are recognizable enough that a number of books have been written about predictable "passages" and "life crises," the especially critical times in the course of any existence. But no one knows exactly when these crises will occur or, more important, precisely what to do about them.

What to do about them is up to each individual. The important thing is to be sensitive to change. And when change does creep up on you, it is essential to be armed with the insight that (if you use this book constructively) can be achieved in order to deal with new problems and new challenges.

The first requisite is to know when change is upon you. This is the test that many people flunk.

Failing the change test

Here are some homely (real) examples of people who were deaf, dumb, and blind to new circumstances and new needs in their lives.

1. The first case may seem trivial but it suggests deeper problems unrecognized. Mark and Laura bought their first station wagon when the children were small, ideal for bedding down youngsters on long trips, for carrying family luggage, for hauling materials for do-it-yourself home improvement projects. Recently they went shopping for a new station wagon because the current one was beginning to give them lots of trouble. They agonized over the high prices. "But station wagons are ideal for us!" they moaned.

   Amazingly, Laura and Mark failed to note that the "children" are 15 and 17. They hardly ever go anywhere with their parents anymore. Home improvement projects are a thing of the past. A smaller car would really be better now. Nevertheless, they bought the station wagon.

2. Here is someone everybody will recognize. Sixty-five-year-old Jonas Smith is a wealthy man. But he still keeps himself and his wife on a tight budget. He grew up during the depression of the 1930s. His father was jobless for a long time. Every penny counted. Jonas still feels poor. He gets very little pleasure out of his wealth. His wife and he quarrel constantly over her "extravagant" tastes. He will leave a fine estate. And a rich widow who may not mourn him too much.

3. Ah, nostalgia. (This example is like the woman who still dresses like a 17-year-old, though she is now 47.) Vincent K. and his wife, Maria, just bought another house after selling their new condominium.

   "That townhouse was too sleek and modern," Mrs. K. complains.

"This home is the real thing. It reminds me of the house I grew up in."

The trouble is, the "new" place is big, old-fashioned, not in the best of condition, and as inappropriate as Mrs. K.'s family home would have been for two empty-nesters who are both working full-time. Neither Vincent nor Maria has the time or the energy to spend on the inefficient "new" place. Keeping up the garden alone is an impossible chore. They took a step backward into the past. They don't realize it yet, but the townhouse was where they really belonged.

4. A common case is that of Doctor Fred S. He works five days a week, is on call the other two. He suffers from hypertension. He is growing careless in his diagnoses. He is too tired to keep up on medical literature. His wife isn't too happy, either. All the years of family neglect have deepened her discontent and alienation. Nevertheless, the good doctor remains a workaholic, endangering his domestic life, his patients, and his physical well-being.

Remap!

Instances like these could be multiplied indefinitely. We all make assumptions, construct elaborate though half-conscious belief systems, based on how things were at an earlier stage of our lives. Conditions change, but we don't. We ignore the volatility of life. We go on paying tribute to outdated beliefs and living according to obsolete patterns. What we do, in effect, is to use an old map to find our way around a city that has acquired new streets, new freeways, new buildings, and new neighborhoods. And then we wonder why we're lost! When this happens, we need to remap—to regeneralize our lives.

How will you know that your future problems relate to failure to recognize change and to regeneralize? We offer a new pencil-and-paper tool that rarely fails to work when a person is feeling unhappy and isn't sure just what the trouble is. This "game" is called EIAG, an acronym for Experience, Identify, Analyze, Generalize. Making regular use of this technique in the future, whenever problems crop up, will help you discover your outdated assumptions about the territory in which you conduct your life. It will uncover new, up-to-date information about the terrain. You will be helped to see what has happened to change you or your environment. And you will be able to draw a new map to bring your life up to date. Making such adjustments is an art form—the art of living.

Using EIAG

Here is how you use EIAG.

Take pencil and paper. Or typewriter, if that suits you better.

1. Write one paragraph, or two at the most, about an *experience* that has troubled you. An argument with your spouse. A disappointing date with a man who turned out to be gay. A troubling incident at work. A miserable evening at a party. A frustrating board meeting. Just describe what happened. No need to use complete sentences. All you need is to make it intelligible to you.

For example: *My husband and I had an unpleasant disagreement the other night. Not quite a quarrel. Well, OK, it was a small quarrel. We were having a drink before dinner. I was telling him about something that happened to me that day. Just as I was working up to the point of the story, he got that glazed look on his face that he often gets and he said: "Hadn't we better go eat dinner? We'll miss the news on Channel 5." I was furious that he interrupted and wasn't paying attention to what I was saying. I got so mad I wouldn't talk to him. We ate dinner in total silence. It wasn't until the news was half over that I thought, "Oh, hell, it's not that important," and I started to talk to him again.*

2. *Identify* the important elements of the episode. Write them down.

For example: *He wasn't paying attention to me. I felt hurt and discounted. I wanted to get back at him. So I punished him by my silence. And I punished myself, because it was so unpleasant.*

3. *Analyze* what was at the bottom of this unresolved episode. Look at the problem not only from your point of view but also from the other person's (or people's) point of view. Were there any false assumptions on your part or theirs? What do you want? How do you propose to get it? Did your behavior during the episode advance your goals, just leave the situation as it was, or make it worse?

For example: *This is an old problem. He has done this to me before—many times. He sometimes interrupts guests, too, which is extremely embarrassing. I think he really isn't aware of what he is doing; his mind wanders away from the subject. As for me, I hate to be ignored and to feel what I have to say isn't important. It seems to reflect on our relationship—it makes me feel inferior, as if he thinks I'm a bit of fluff. I think I'm just as smart as he is. But I*

*guess what be does isn't meant to put me down. He just isn't
thinking. The trouble is, I've never had it out with him. I just suffer,
or get silent. I really didn't want to make a big deal out of a little
thing. But because this problem keeps happening and because I
draw such terrible conclusions from his behavior—that I am devalued, inferior, etc.—maybe we should discuss it?*

4. *Generalize* from the experience. Work out a new rule of behavior,
a new point of view, that should stand you in good stead for this
problem and for similar problems in the future.

For example: *Now I realize that I usually avoid arguments. When I
was a kid my mother forbade me to fight with my brother. During
the early years of our marriage I lived by the rule of not arguing
with my husband because the children might hear. What I really
should do is recognize that everything is different now. My mother
is dead. I'm grown up. The children are gone. No one can hear us
argue. And it doesn't even need to be a fight. Why can't I just come
out with what I want? I should tell him once and for all how I feel
about this kind of treatment. I should hear his side of it, too. I have
to ask for what I want—and clear the air once and for all.*

Outdated behavior

This homely marital example illustrates an important principle: that
lives keep changing and circumstances keep changing, that behavior
that once worked doesn't work anymore. By taking a thoughtful look
at a distressing incident, using the EIAG technique, this woman discovered that she was no longer a child, bound to obey the strictures of
mother; that she was no longer a young mother, bound to consider her
children's welfare more important than her own; that even a 25-year-
old marriage can stand refurbishing.

Sometimes behavior on the job needs refurbishing, too. One of the
authors of this book, a college professor, had a distressing classroom
experience. His teaching style has always been informal, unorthodox,
indirect, not traditional, but generally successful. Also, students know
that he is approachable at any time, in class and outside classroom
hours. So it was hardly unusual when, at the end of the semester, a
member of an advanced class in business management asked for a
conference. This time the reason was a complaint.

"I don't feel that I've learned anything from you," the professor was
told. "I'm used to classroom lectures, taking notes, doing the reading,

studying, and then taking a midterm and a final. I like to know where the course is going and what I am supposed to have learned. But your methods are so—well, crazy—and I'm afraid I'll flunk. It's so disorganized. I don't understand you or the subject matter of the course. You don't even give a final. How can I put it all together?"

The professor was distressed enough by this interview to use his own prescribed tool, EIAG, to analyze the experience.

Experience: *The student complained that his learning style and my teaching style were incompatible. The class was too unstructured. He didn't learn, he said.*

Identify: *I don't* feel *nontraditional. I ask for two papers during the semester. Many other professors rely on papers and don't give exams. This student actually wrote excellent papers. They showed that he learned a great deal. I told him so. Still, he doesn't feel satisfied. And neither do I. I'd like all students to realize how much they really got out of my course.*

Analyze: *I have been taking it for granted that everybody understands what I'm getting at. I try to help these adult students to dig out the principles of business management from their own experience — it should mean more that way. But this individual didn't realize that I act as a catalyzing agent for each member of my class, so that each will learn from his own experience.*

Generalize: *I realize that I have enjoyed being the magician who pulls rabbits out of hats. I like my role of being someone who surprises the class by being nondirective and letting them think they found out everything by themselves. I suppose I glory in my low-key stance. A bit of ego there? That student is probably not unique. Others must have felt the same way. In future, I am going to have to explain in advance what my teaching style is intended to accomplish. It will take some of the fun out of it for me but it's not fair to the many literal-minded, traditional-minded members of my classes.*

The moral of this particular EIAG is that nobody — even college professors, even human behavior specialists — is immune from the need to make behavioral changes.

For you, in the future, EIAG, as well as other "tests" and devices described in the chapters you have already read, should be a means of keeping up with the changes and new problems in your life. From these structured reexperiences, enabling you to get in touch with your inner selves, you will achieve insight. You will be helped to understand how you are keeping yourself from self-fulfillment. You will be able to define your real current problem(s), to analyze them both intuitively and with the use of reason. Relying on your own heretofore hidden inner resources, you will develop new alternatives, in order to create practical ways of solving your dilemma. You will go forward happily and constructively — at least until the next cycle of your life requires new adaptations and new solutions.

Write yourself a letter

For now, to tie down your gains at this juncture in your life, why not write yourself a letter summarizing what you have learned as a result of carrying out the suggestions in the preceding chapters? To inspire you, here is such a letter written by someone who was willing to share his own life crisis and the solution he worked out to solve his problem.

The "subject" is a male, a successful retail businessman who owned two stores. At 40, he suffered a mild heart attack. The physical crisis gave him a period of enforced leisure and an impetus to confront, at long last, his mid-life spiritual crisis. Note that the writer of this letter conscientiously followed the suggestions for self-analysis and inner communion laid out in each chapter of this book. As a result, he emerged with a map showing the path to self-fulfillment.

Yes, I did make a survey of my life. And I'm delighted to report that, at last, I faced my problem. I confronted the fact that I had become a businessman chiefly because that was the family pattern, what my father expected. It was a way of earning the kind of income that allowed me to provide my own family with household help, country club membership, and a secure place in the upper middle class. But I had been denying the stress that led to my heart attack. The truth was that I disliked merchandising and selling. I loved to read and to study. Business victories were unsatisfying. Learning (sneaked into my daily schedule) was the real thrill. What I really wanted was to go back to graduate school and get my intellectual credentials.

I learned to trust myself, to accept that I had the guts and the ability to make this revolutionary change without tearing up my family or myself.

Finally, at 40, I owned myself. I accepted the scholar in me, conceded that as a retailer I was misplaced. I was not my father's little boy. I was me, different, for better or for worse.

I made an agreement with myself to accept the responsibility for my own actions, and to take a considerable risk: to seek a fellowship at the state university, to sell my stores, to use the proceeds to support my family while I was in school, to risk the disapproval of my father and my wife.

I analyzed the mind-set that had, until then, frozen me into the role of businessman. I realized that I had been competing with my father on his terms; I had had the conviction that success could only be achievement as previously defined by my family. I realized that I had imposed my inappropriate life on myself, by swallowing the childish notion that I must match or outdo my father. I learned that I needed to discard that mind-set and become me — not him.

My life, I decided, had become totally lopsided. Of course I needed to support my family. But I also needed to support my personal requirement to live the life of a scholar. By becoming a scientist, eventually I would be able to do both: earn a reasonable salary; live a life of the mind and enjoy my occupation.

My alternatives became clearer. I could opt to do research, perhaps also to teach. I could ask my wife to help support the family. I could go to school part-time. I might go into a different, more "intellectual" sort of business.

I worked out a whole new regeneralization for my life. For my physical and mental health, I must be myself (not my father). I must find fulfillment in my own kind of work. I am no businessman. I owe my family support but I also owe myself a certain degree of fulfillment. I must change careers now.

And so he did. And lived happily ever after? Let us say—because it is true—that he was indeed much happier after he had come to terms with his inner self and had had the courage to make the necessary changes in his occupational life. But other aspects of his existence needed new attention as the years rolled on. There came a time when his marriage became a source of considerable emotional turmoil. It was necessary to deal with that. New career dissatisfaction appeared. Again, it was necessary to go through appropriate self-analysis and soul-searching. New individuals became meaningful to him and again the delicate balance of his existence had to be readjusted. The children grew up. An aged parent—that selfsame father—needed and demanded attention. These changes precipitated new crises, new challenges, renewed need to sort through personal spiritual resources and to listen to inner voices.

Was this man's life ever free of turmoil? Yes—for considerable periods it was happy, productive, and rewarding. But at various times, because that is the human condition, he needed to confront problems and to work out ways of solving those problems, ways that were uniquely right for him.

What you have learned

We have now reached the last pages of this book called THE ART OF SELF-FULFILLMENT. As the two authors wrote, they lived the book themselves, conscientiously reapplying its principles to their own lives and carrying out yet again its various exercises, taking once more the prescribed tests. The reader has no doubt already suspected that some of the "examples" relate to the authors themselves.

Yes, the authors did use themselves for illustrative purposes, but they also used (in discreet disguise) case histories in the persons of many individuals encountered during years of professional experience. Thus they reaffirmed the validity of the systems they have prescribed for you, the reader, to help you gain awareness and insight in order to achieve greater self-fulfillment.

What you have learned in the course of these chapters is that there is no quick fix for the problems and difficulties that beset all people in the course of their lives. Rather, you have been given a *process*, an ever-adaptable mechanism for dealing with the trials and tribulations and problems of daily life. Never forget that you can be your own worst enemy—but also your own most creative ally. You have the tools. Use them whenever you feel restless, unhappy, unfulfilled.

Good luck! Have a good life!

Bibliography

Bandler, Richard, and Grinder, John, *The Structure of Magic*. Science and Behavior Books, Palo Alto, 1975.

Bandler, Grinder, and Satir, Virginia, *Changing with Families*. Science and Behavior Books, Palo Alto, 1976.

Bateson, Gregory, *Steps to an Ecology of Mind*. Ballantine Books, New York, 1972.

Edwards, Betty, *Drawing on the Right Side of the Brain*. Houghton Mifflin, Boston, 1979.

Erickson, Milton H., *The Nature of Hypnosis and Suggestion*. Irvington Publishers, New York, 1980.

Feldenkrais, Moshe, *Awareness through Movement: Health Exercises for Personal Growth*. Harper and Row, New York, 1972.

Annual Handbook for Group Facilitators. University Associates Inc. San Diego (yearly).

Lilly, John, and Lilly, Antonietta, *The Dyadic Cyclone*. Pocket Books, New York, 1977.

Progoff, Ira, *At a Journal Workshop*. Dialogue House Library, New York, 1975.

Simon, Sidney B., *Meeting Yourself Halfway*. Argus Communications, Niles, Illinois, 1974.